MODERN

HIGH CHURCH PRINCIPLES

EXAMINED:

AS EXHIBITED IN THE

"TRACTS FOR THE TIMES;"

ESPECIALLY THOSE WRITTEN BY

THE REV. PROFESSOR PUSEY,

CANON OF CHRIST CHURCH, OXFORD, &c.

LONDON:

PUBLISHED BY L. AND G. SEELEY, FLEET STREET;
SOLD BY NISBET AND CO., BERNERS STREET.

1837.

MACINTOSH, PRINTER,
GREAT NEW STREET, LONDON.

ADVERTISEMENT.

THE following observations on the *Tracts for the Times,* originally appeared in the *Record* newspaper. They are now published in their present form, at the request of many of the readers of that journal.

The reference to the sentiments of the early Fathers of the Church, on one of the subjects most carefully discussed by the Oxford Divines, is necessarily imperfect. Within limits so circumscribed, it was impossible fully to discuss or illustrate the subject. So far, however, as it is treated of, it is hoped the effect will be salutary. The Reverend Gentleman by whom that chapter is written, has been long and intimately acquainted with the works of the Fathers; and it is his settled judgment that a full examination into their entire writings, would issue in no dissimilar result to that stated in the following pages.

London, January 25, 1837.

TABLE OF CONTENTS.

CHAPTER I.

CHAPTER II.

CHAPTER III.

CHAPTER IV.

CHAPTER V.

CHAPTER VI.

CHAPTER VII.

CHAPTER VIII.

HIGH CHURCH PRINCIPLES,

&c. &c.

CHAPTER I.

ILLUSTRATED BY THE ROMISH APOSTACY.

BEING disposed to make some observations on what are designated High Church Principles, as at present exhibited in the Church of England, we first inquire what is the import of the term. It appears to be expressive of a class of opinions which affect to lodge powers and attribute properties to the visible Church, and particularly to the Sacraments as administered by her, beyond those with which she is invested by her Great Head, as declared in the Inspired Volume.

The most striking example of these principles is exhibited by the Romish Apostacy. And, if we mistake not, a reference to that community will cast considerable light on the entire subject. That " Mystery of Iniquity" already wrought in the Apostolic age. It appears to have had its foundation in the leading sin of angel and man—pride; and to have led to a thirst for self-exaltation, personal pre-eminence, and the possession of power, dignity, and glory. Human power, professing to have only earthly origin, has sometimes been tremendously great. But the power after which Rome aspired, and to which she attained was above and beyond all this. She grasped Almighty power. The supreme head was infallible. He gave or withheld, not only the treasures and glories of this world, but those of the world to come, by a sovereign sway. He ruled, not only over the outward conduct, but penetrated into the inmost hearts of his subjects. He saw their thoughts. And they could neither speak nor think of God, nor of his revelation, nor of his providence, nor of their relations to him, but as

B

he commanded—those commands being enforced by fire and sword; " so that he, as God, *sat* in the temple of God, showing himself *to be* God." (2 Thes. ii. 4.)

The subsidiary and inferior agents by which he wrought, and insinuated himself into the hearts of his subjects over his expanded empire, were bound to fealty, not only by solemn oaths and the most sacred obligations, but by the most powerful of human motives, self-interest. The gradations by which they might rise from the lowest to the highest situations in the Church, were many, and clearly marked. The Pontifical crown itself glittered in the warm imaginations and before the ardent ambition of thousands who were never to attain to it; while the honour appertaining to all the inferior grades of the clergy, regular and irregular, whether of a secular, ecclesiastical, or spiritual description, or formed by curious and diversified combinations of all three, bound them to the Church by stronger than mere earthly ties, which again were multiplied and twined into unexampled strength by the loss of every thing human and divine, which surely followed on the crime of apostasy. To this unexampled confederacy is to be traced the prostration for so extended a period, even of the worldly liberties of the species. But it was by professing to teach the doctrine of Christ with Apostolic purity and divine authority, while in fact it substituted the commandments of men for the word of God, that Popery reduced the mind under the bondage of an abject and degrading superstition, instead of nurturing it in the glorious liberty of the children of God. It, in short, rendered the doctrines and precepts of revelation of none effect, but it established the authority of the Church on their ruins. In the name of God it cast out God, and accomplished the exaltation of the Church by the abasement of every thing which the Church is constituted to exalt. Here, we say, were exhibited the perfect triumph and full effect of pure High Church principles.

The methods by which the Papacy reduced its subjects under its degrading domination, are obvious as they were diversified, while they all sprang out of this one principle, the infallibility of the Church, and its absolute right to interpret the word, and authoritatively to declare the mind of God. By its traditions it so encompassed its victims, that from the cradle to the grave they could effect no escape from its snares—nay, beyond the grave, and amidst the darkness of an unseen world, it still maintained its grasp upon them, to exasperate, or to moderate or extinguish the fires of Divine wrath, which by its own fiat it enkindled, that by means of them it might give additional energy and extention to its usurped and demoniac authority.

Few people can read with understanding the revelation of Jesus Christ without being struck with the absolute and unqualified freeness of the offers of the Gospel to every human being who shall hear "the glad tidings of great joy." The direction is to preach the Gospel to every creature under heaven, and to offer to him its everlasting treasures without money and without price. Thus the objects of the Christian ministry are to disseminate the truth; and by its dissemination to gather the children of God into one, and to feed them with the bread which came down from heaven, unto eternal life. The object of the institution of the Christian ministry is not certainly to hinder or obstruct the circulation of the knowledge of salvation, but to make its diffusion more rapid and more sure, and to bring home to the bosoms of those who through grace should accept it all its rich provisions, and to enforce upon them all its sacred obligations.

The Papacy, however, wrested all the ordinances and privileges of the Gospel (putting them under greater or less constraint, as the case required) for its own aggrandisement, and the establishment of its own power.

Free access to God, by PRAYER, granted to every human being whom the Gospel shall reach, connected with the promise and oath of God, that the suppliant so coming shall in no wise be cast out, but shall receive every thing necessary to his full and everlasting salvation, may be considered the leading privilege obtained for the world through the death and advocacy of Christ. Now the freeness with which this privilege is offered, and the fulness of the promises by which it is secured to every one that heareth and accepteth of it, are beyond all adequate description. But the Papacy here stepped in, and for her own personal exaltation, and the more sure fastening of her yoke of bondage on her slaves, deprived these offers, in effect, of all their freeness and all their fulness. It did this in various ways; but by none more immediately or effectually than by this dogma—that confession of sin, to be accepted by God, must be made to the priest: that till such confession to the priest is made, sin must remain uncancelled; and that it is only removed when the priest pronounces the absolution. By this act, for the gratification of her High Church propensities—with a view to secure to herself more than is given her, she absolutely comes between God and the sinner, and teaches that till she is satisfied God is addressed in vain. Daring impiety! Wickedness truly enormous!

The charter of our spiritual privileges is the BIBLE, to open which is graciously permitted to every creature under heaven. But the

Papacy closes the book. She does this because the revelation of the mind and will of God is inconsistent with the power which she assumes, and the dogmas which she teaches. Her pretence is, that the free perusal of the word of God would endanger men's eternal salvation (how impious is the allegation). And here again God's word is cast out, that her power may stand.

The SACRAMENTS have been vouchsafed for the instruction, edification, and consolation of the Church. Baptism is " a *sign* of Regeneration, or new birth, whereby, as by an instrument, they that receive Baptism rightly, are grafted into the Church. (Art. 27.) In the Lord's Supper, " the body of Christ is given, taken, and eaten only after an heavenly and spiritual manner; and the mean whereby the body of Christ is received and eaten in the Supper, is faith." (Art. 28.) Not to dwell on the other Sacraments which the Papal Church has instituted, she identifies the act of Baptism with that new creation of the soul by God, which is the sole prerogative of the Almighty; and which identification, the carnal, unenlightened, worldly, and depraved state of the great mass of her followers, in all ages, would prove (were other proofs wanting) to be a vain and wicked thing; while, in the Sacrament of the Supper, she changes the spiritual feeding by faith on Christ, as the bread of life, into an actual distribution by the Church of the real flesh and blood of Christ! Here, again, we mark how all is made to concentrate on the same one point—the exaltation of the Church—the investing her with powers altogether prodigious and preternatural, for the establishment and enforcement of her unrighteous domination.

And so if we look to the other errors and false assumptions of the Papacy, what do they all tend to, but to the increase and enlargement of her power? Besides Christ, other *mediators or intercessors*, in whom she has a peculiar propriety, and over whom she exercises a peculiar influence. *Salvation by works*, and her treasury of *works, of supererogation*, whence she dispenses to those who lack, and delivers the souls in purgatory from their fiery trial. *Purgatory. Fasts;* and *indulgence from fasting. Indulgences* not only for sins past, but for sins to be committed. What do we see, in all such dogmas and deceits of the Papal Church, but means of increasing her power—of usurping authority which Christ never granted her—and by this means of gratifying the most general propensity and vice of human nature?

In the Papacy we thus see the character of High Church principles fully developed. The object of the Christian ministry and of the Apostolic Church is, to preach the Gospel to every creature to hold forth the lamp of revelation for their own illumination, and for the direction of a lost world into the path of peace. They will do so with just effect, under the blessing of God, by assuming no more than the powers with which they are invested by the Great Head of the Church, and using only the scriptural weapons which he has put into their hands. But the Papacy sought its own, not the things of Christ Jesus. It usurped powers with which he had never invested it. With a view to its own exaltation and aggrandizement, it has dared to close the Book of Life,—it has ventured to interpose itself between the sinner, and his Saviour and God,—and it has not ceased till it has perverted the Gospel, and become the minister of Satan instead of the ambassador of God.

Let us mark in this progress and consummation of Popery, the danger of going beyond the limits which Scripture has assigned to the Church. Such powers as are clearly proved from Scripture to appertain to her, ought to be freely and firmly exercised; but the assumption by her of powers derived from any other quarter, and not resting on that one foundation, whether they affect the matter of the Gospel, its promulgation, the privileges of professing Christians, or of mankind at large, ought to be viewed with extreme jealousy. And this not the less so when the character of those who make suspicious or dangerous pretensions is unexceptionable, and their motives good and praiseworthy. No one with even the slightest acquaintance with the history of Popery can doubt, that while the mere love of power and aggrandizement lay at the root of its main corruptions and perversions of the revelation of God, and by its constant operation brought them to baneful maturity, multitudes of those nursed in them, most firmly believed in their correspondence with truth, and with the will of God, and considered they did God service even when they persecuted his saints to the death. And so now, the fact of many in our own Church who are busy nursing fresh shoots, as we verily believe, from the same root, being respectable, conscientious, and well-intentioned persons, should, far from laying our suspicions, only awaken us to additional zeal in marking the real nature and probable consequences of their operations. The Church has seldom so much occasion to dread *outward* evils as those which originate *within* her, and are fostered by her professed friends. All experience teaches this truth, and let not our experience be of no avail in the present day.

Having by these observations cleared our ground—having endeavoured to define in what, according to our views, High Church principles consist, namely, in the assumption by the Church of *higher* powers and prerogatives than those with which Scripture invests her, and having glanced at the striking example exhibited by the Romish Church of the destruction and ruin in which such assumptions in their maturity may issue, we purpose in the next Chapter to proceed to test by Scripture some of the pretensions and assumptions of the High Church party in our own day and in our own Church, in the hope of discovering and deciding whether or not they are in conformity with the word and will of God. " To the law and to the testimony: if they speak not according to this word, it is because there is no light in them." (Is. viii. 20.)

CHAPTER II.

THE APOSTOLICAL SUCCESSION.

HAVING attempted to define the term *High Church*, and presented it in its full stature as exhibited by the Romish apostacy, we now proceed to examine the character of the principles to which the same term is generally affixed in our own Communion, with the view of discovering whether or not they are coincident with the Word of God. We undertake the task under a deep sense of its necessity. We believe those principles are spreading with a blighting effect over many an otherwise fair corner of the Lord's vineyard. And whatever others may do, we, at least, shall minister our feeble help, as God shall enlighten and strengthen us, to place them in the light of Scripture. If they stand that light, let them be further circulated and made known: if they be found wanting, let them be cast out of the household of Faith. And we beseech all those who shall find what we advance on the subject opposed to their preconceived opinions, to consider our observations with candour and with prayer. We can appeal to God that our desire is to establish HIS truth, and that alone ; and it is our prayer that whatever we may advance in opposition to his revealed will may be utterly dissipated and lost.

. It is first necessary to exhibit the description of opinion in our own Church, which is generally denominated High Church. We define High Church principles as those which would lodge power in, and attribute properties to the visible Church, and especially to the

Sacraments as administered by her, beyond and above those with which she is invested by the Great Head of the Church, as declared by the Scriptures; and if we now give illustrations of these principles as maintained by members of our communion, nothing will be wanting to enable the reader to see with distinctness those things against which we contend.

The following extracts we take from a series of Essays, called *Tracts for the Times*, written by men of high name and character at Oxford. The publication of them is still proceeding in monthly numbers, and those for 1833 — 5 have aleady been collected in two handsome octavo volumes. A very few specimens will be amply sufficient for our immediate purpose.

In the first volume, No. 10, we find the following passages :—

" But, it may be asked, are these spiritual sons of the Apostles still alive? No : all this took place many hundred years ago. These sons and heirs of the Apostles died long since. But then they in turn did not leave the world without committing their sacred office to a fresh set of ministers, and they in turn to another, and so on, even to this day. Thus the Apostles had, first, spiritual sons ; then spiritual grandsons ; then great-grandsons ; and so on, from one age to another, down to the present time. . . . *(Of course the Pope was the most illustrious of all these descendants.)*

" And so, in just the same way, though for much higher reasons, we must honour the Bishop, because he *is* the Bishop ;—for his *office*-sake ; because he is Christ's minister,—stands in the place of the Apostles,—is the Shepherd of our souls on earth, while Christ is away. This is faith, to look at things not as seen, but as unseen ; to be as sure that the Bishop is Christ's appointed representative, as if we actually saw him work miracles as St. Peter and St. Paul did, as you may read in the book of the Acts of the Apostles. . . . . *(The Pope never asked for stronger faith than this.)*

" Thus the whole plan of salvation hangs together. Christ the true Mediator above ; His servant, the Bishop, His earthly likeness ; (*consider the Pope in this light*) mankind the subjects of his teaching ; God the author of his salvation. . . .

" Then you will honour us, with a purer honour than many men do now, namely, as those (if I may say so) who are intrusted with the keys of heaven and hell, as the heralds of mercy, as the denouncers of wo to wicked men, as intrusted with the awful and mysterious privilege of dispensing Christ's body and blood, as far greater than the most powerful and the wealthiest of men in our unseen strength and our heavenly riches."

In No. 4, of the same volume, p. 5, the following passage occurs :—

" Why should we talk so much of an *Establishment*, and so little of an Apostolical Succession ? Why should we not seriously endeavour to impress our people with this plain truth,—that by separating themselves from our communion, they separate themselves not only from a decent, orderly, useful society, but from THE ONLY CHURCH IN THIS REALM WHICH HAS A RIGHT TO BE QUITE SURE THAT SHE HAS THE LORD'S BODY TO GIVE TO HIS PEOPLE?"

In No. 15, page 2, there is the following passage :—

"You may observe, that our Lord himself did not preach the Gospel, without proving most plainly that HIS FATHER had sent Him. He and His Apostles prove their Divine commission by miracles. As miracles, however, have long ago come to an end, there must be some *other* way for a man to prove his right to be a minister of religion. And what *other way can there possibly be,* except a regular call and ordination by those who have succeeded to the Apostles?" (*The Popish Priests have this indisputably, which is not quite the case with our Oxford brethren. Had we not better go at once to Rome, that we may be quite sure?*)

So much as to the powers and prerogatives of those endowed with the Apostolical Succession. As it regards those who are supposed to want it, it is said in the same Number (15), page 3 :—

"Surely those who dissent from the Church have *invented* an ordinance, as they themselves must allow; whereas Churchmen, whether rightly or wrongly, still maintain *their* succession not to be an invention, but to be God's ordinance. If Dissenters say, that *order* requires there should be some such *succession,* this is true, indeed, but still it is only a testimony to the mercy of Christ, in having, as Churchmen maintain, *given us* such a succession. And this is *all* it shows; it does nothing for *them.*"

On the same subject it is observed in Number 35, p. 3 :—

"A person not commissioned from the Bishop, may use the words of Baptism, and sprinkle or bathe with the water, *on earth,* but there is no promise from Christ, that such a man shall admit souls to the *kingdom of heaven.* A person not commissioned may break bread, and pour out wine, and pretend to give the Lord's Supper, but it can afford no comfort to any to receive it at his hands, because there is no warrant from Christ to lead communicants to suppose that while he does so here *on earth,* they will be partakers in the Saviour's heavenly body and blood. And as for the person himself, who takes upon himself without warrant to minister in holy things, he is all the while treading in the footsteps of Korah, Dathan, and Abiram, whose awful punishment you read of in the book of Numbers. (Compare Numbers xvi. with Jude ver. 11.)

And again at the last page of the same Number:—

"Learn, then, to cherish and value the blessing which God has vouchsafed to you, in having given you pastors who have received this commission. *The Dissenting teachers have it not.* They lay no claim to regular succession from the Apostles; and though the Roman Catholic clergy have indeed been ordained by the hands of Bishops, they are mere intruders in this country, have no right to come here, and besides, have so corrupted the truth of God's word, that they are not to be listened to for a moment."

In Number 40, we find two passages of Scripture thus rendered:—

"St. Matt. xxviii. 19.

"If you would be a disciple, or Christian, you must be baptized by Apostolical authority in the name of the Holy Trinity."

"St. Matt. xxvi. 28.

"If you would eat Christ's body and drink his blood, you must take and eat the bread and drink of the cup, blessed by those who have authority to bless it, in remembrance of Him."

Some of the practical advantages to be derived from such instruction is summed up in the advertisement prefixed to the volume in the following words at page 4 :—

"Had he (the sinner), been taught as a child, that the sacraments, not preaching, are the sources of Divine grace ; that the Apostolical ministry had a virtue in it which went out over the whole Church, when sought by the prayer of faith ; that fellowship with it was a gift and privilege, as well as a duty, we could not have had so many wanderers from our fold, nor so many cold hearts within it."

The following passage is so fully descriptive of the views of these writers, that we shall extract it from the advertisement affixed to the second volume :—

"For example, would not most men maintain, on the first view of the subject, that to administer the Lord's Supper to infants, or to the dying and insensible, however consistently pious and believing in their past lives, was a superstition? *and yet both practices have the sanction of primitive usage.* And does not this account for the prevailing indisposition to admit that Baptism conveys regeneration? Indeed, this may even be set down as the essence of sectarian doctrine (however its mischief may be restrained or compensated, in the case of individuals), to consider faith, and not the Sacraments, as the *instrument of justification* and other Gospel gifts; instead of holding that the grace of Christ comes to us altogether from without, (as from Him, so through externals of His ordaining,) faith being but the *sine qua non*, the necessary condition on our parts for duly receiving it."

The same set of opinions are taught in the following lines, which we extract from the *British Magazine* for August last, in which our readers will perceive the members of the Church of Scotland, generally, are counted as idolators, and given over to the uncovenanted mercies of God :—

"SAMARIA.

"O rail not at our brethren of the North,
Albeit Samaria finds her likeness there ;—
A self-form'd Priesthood, and the Church cast forth,
To the chill mountain air.

" What, though their Fathers sinned, and lost the grace
Which seals the holy Apostolic line?
Christ's love o'erflows the bounds his Prophets trace,
In his unveil'd design.

" Israel had seers: to them the word is nigh;
Shall not that word run forth, and gladness give,
To many a Shunamite, till in his eye,
The full seven thousand live?"

Passages of a similar tendency as the above, though not so broadly expressed, are to be found in abundance in the pages of the *British Magazine;* which publication, most of our readers are aware, makes very extraordinary assumptions of Orthodoxy, while it is under the management of a well-known member of our Church.

While the *British Magazine* thus cuts off from the communion of the faithful the Church of Scotland, that distinguished, faithful, and highly-honoured child of the Reformation, it thus lovingly speaks of the works and services of "the Mother of Abominations "—

" O, that thy creed were sound,
For thou dost soothe the heart, thou Church of Rome,
By thy unwearied watch, and varied round
Of service, *in thy Saviour's* HOLY HOME.

" I cannot walk the city's sultry streets,
But the wide porch invites to still retreats,
Where Passion's thirst is calmed, and Care's unthankful gloom."

British Magazine, February, 1836.

Such being the sentiments under examination, and such some of their practical results, we shall at present consider the question of the *Apostolical Succession,* on which they mainly rest, and deprived of which, the greater part of their other objectionable positions are greatly weakened, or fall to the ground.

These writers being all by profession attached members and dutiful sons of the Church of England, it may be well to inquire, in the first place, what is the judgment of the Church on the subject? It is not necessary to go far, or to seek carefully, for her decision, for one of her Articles is devoted to a settlement of the question, Who are authorized to assume " the office of public preaching, or ministering the sacraments in the congregation?" If these Reverend members of our communion, therefore, instead of digging into the deeps of Popery, or into those " primitive," but most superstitious times, when the Lord's Supper was administered " to infants and to the insensible," would listen to the scriptural exposition and decision of the question by her whose children they profess to be, we should have a speedy end put to such lucubrations as those which we have been constrained to bring under the notice of our readers.

In the 23d Article, entitled " Of ministering in the congregation," the Church says :—" It is not lawful for any man to take upon him the office of public preaching, or ministering the sacraments in the congregation before he be lawfully called and sent to execute the same." So far the Church and the Oxford brethren are agreed. The next question is, who are lawfully called? This question the Church decides in the following words:—" *And those we ought to judge lawfully called and sent, which be chosen and called to this work by men who have public authority given unto them in the congregation to call and send ministers into the Lord's vineyard.*"

How wise, catholic, and comprehensive is this announcement of our Church on the subject we shall have occasion presently to consider. But let our readers mark, that not a single word is said, in direct terms, of that "holy Apostolic line," without which there is only, according to our Oxford brethren, " a self-formed priesthood," a second " Samaria," and a people left to the uncovenanted mercies of God. They fix upon this point as *fundamental*—as that upon which the Church must *rest for security* in every trial. The Church herself, far from being the source whence these her children draw those extreme and extravagant opinions, says not a word to which not only the Protestant Continental Churches, and the Church of Scotland could not subscribe, but to which all the respectable Dissenting bodies in the kingdom would not also set their seal. Our brethren, we perceive, talk much of sectarianism. In this matter is it they, or their Church, that is sectarian? Her language is that of union. Theirs, on the contrary, is the language of division and separation; and they are led into this crooked and unchristian path (in opposition to the guidance of their Church, which they were bound to follow), by embracing, as we shall presently see, the shadow instead of the substance of religion—by mistaking the outward body and framework, for the spirit of Christianity.

We turn next to Scripture,—for " whatsoever is not read therein or may be proved thereby, is not to be required of any man that it should be believed as an article of the faith." (Sixth Article.)

We assert, then, without reserve or hesitation, that there is no ground in Scripture upon which to rest the dogma of the Apostolical Succession, as held and explained by the Oxford brethren.

To establish their position, they must prove from Holy Scripture four things. 1. That our Lord ordained Apostles, giving them powers to ordain other men to preach the Gospel, and so forward to the end of time. 2. That He or his inspired Apostles anathematised all others, who, under any conceivable circumstances, attempted, or should attempt, to preach the Gospel or administer the Sacraments. 3. That the command given to commit THE TRUTH " to *faithful* men who should be able to teach others also," held good for the great purposes for which the Christian ministry was established, although *unfaithful* men were ordained instead of "*faithful*," who should teach the doctrines of devils instead of the truth of God. 4. That no power is reserved to the members of the Church, in the event of " another Gospel" being preached by those outwardly ordained, instead of the Gospel of Christ, of throwing off the ministers of Satan, and placing over the faithful, true men who should lead them in the right way. We repeat, that unless our Oxford brethren can make good these four propositions, their theory on the subject cannot stand. To the *first* we all subscribe. The *second* is plainly contrary to Scripture. The *third* is equally so. And the *fourth* is also altogether opposed to the spirit of the Gospel, repudiated by its letter, contrary to that common sense of mankind to which so many appeals are made in the Word of God, while it is proved to be false by the history of the Church. If we make good these assertions, we shall prove that our Oxford brethren would not only have been better Churchmen, but better Christians, had they humbly submitted themselves in these matters to the guidance of their Church, instead of casting from them her venerable authority, and pursuing their investigations even in those " primitive times " when the Sacrament of the Supper was administered to unconscious infants.

The *first* point being disposed of by universal admission, we proceed to the consideration of the *second ;* and we shall prove that there is no warrant in Scripture for anathematising those who preach the Gospel, on account of their supposed want of Apostolical authority. Every man of ordinary understanding must perceive that the acknowledgment of the indisputable fact, that Christ made due provision for the regular administration of the Word and Sacrament, is a thing as distinct as possible from cursing those who may dispense them, not having this authority. And if it can be shown, from Holy Writ, that those who, in our Lord's and the Apostles' times, ventured upon the work of the ministry, not only without ordination, but who prosecuted it under unjustifiable circumstances, were not anathematised, were not even forbidden ; *a fortiori*, they are not to be anathematised or forbidden, who enter on the work of the ministry out of " the Apostolic line," in circumstances in which it was impossible to maintain that line without denying the Gospel, and who entered it, not with an evil spirit, but in the spirit of martyrs and confessors, and whose labours, and those of their successors, the Lord has blessed with abundant success in the building up of his spiritual temple.

There were those in the time of our Lord who absolutely abstained from approaching the Prince of Life, seeing in Him no form or comeliness, who yet not only preached Christ, but absolutely "cast out devils in his name." The disciples forbade them, because they followed not them. The Saviour said, "FORBID THEM NOT." This Scripture "is written for our learning."

When a prisoner at Rome, the Apostle thus writes to the Philippians:—" And MANY of the brethren in the Lord, waxing confident by my bonds, are much more bold to speak the word without fear. Some indeed preach Christ even of envy and strife; and some also of good-will; the one preach Christ of contention, not sincerely, supposing to add affliction to my bonds; but the other of love, knowing that I am set for the defence of the Gospel. What, then? notwithstanding every way, whether in pretence, or in truth, Christ is preached; and I therein do rejoice, yea, and will rejoice."

Is it reasonably to be supposed that the MANY brethren who, according to this passage, "*preached Christ*," "of love," and over whom the Apostle rejoiced, were "ordained" ministers? We think not. But assuredly those who did so "of envy and strife" were not so. And yet the blessed Apostle, instead of comparing even men who, by their malignant preaching of Christ, sought to "add affliction to his bonds," to Korah and his Company, as our Oxford brethren do all who under any circumstances are out of "the holy Apostolic line," only says, "What then? Notwithstanding every way, whether in pretence or in truth Christ is preached; and I therein do rejoice, yea, and will rejoice." How different, then, must we conclude, even from this example, were the principles of the Apostle, and the views which he entertained of the glorious Gospel, from those cherished and promulgated by the Oxford divines. Not that we argue from such passages against a due and becoming order in the Church of God, for that were most unscriptural. "God is not the author of confusion, but of peace," and the exhortation is, "let all things be done decently and in order." But we draw from such premises this obvious conclusion, that if, even in such circumstances, Paul gloried in the preaching of Christ, instead of using his Apostolical authority to close the mouths of the preachers, or devoting them to destruction as Korah, Dathan, and Abiram, how infinitely unbecoming, how wholly unscriptural is such conduct exhibited by our Oxford brethren in regard to men whose predecessors (not themselves) considered themselves impelled either to remain in the idolatries and superstitions of Rome, or cutting off all intercourse with that "Mother of Harlots and Abominations" to preach Christ—not of "envy and strife," but of love, with the Holy Ghost, with much assurance, and to the everlasting salvation of multitudes of immortal souls.

The same view of the subject is confirmed and illustrated by the circumstances under which Apollos began his public ministry, as narrated in the latter part of the 18th chapter of the Acts.

But to advert to the *third* position which we laid down as that which it is necessary for the Oxford divines to establish for the vindication of their theory, what shall we think of "the Holy Apostolic line," not belonging to which, a man is ministering not the Gospel, but standing amidst the uncovenanted mercies of God—nay, worse far than this, is absolutely involved in the condemnation of Korah, Dathan, and Abiram?

"The HOLY Apostolic line," from the days of the Apostles to the present day! Was the line through Popery *holy?* Can a man be "ordained" by God to preach error instead of truth? to preach "*another Gospel*," every individual who does so, being deliberately pronounced by the Apostle, under the plenary inspiration of the Holy Spirit, TO BE ACCURSED? (Gal. i. 8.) Can a man's ordination to administer the Sacraments be ratified of God, who, for the one oblation of Christ, substitutes "the sacrifice of masses" declared by our Church to be "*blasphemous fables?*" Can a man be ordained to deny Christ, and to substitute for the glad tidings of the Gospel the heresies and abominations of the Romish apostacy? Impossible! If "Satan cannot cast out Satan," far less can Christ cast out Christ. The injunction is to commit the glorious Gospel of the grace of God to "faithful men," who should teach others also. But the instant "another Gospel" is substituted for the true Gospel, that moment the man ceases to be the minister of Christ—he is "accursed"—he is not for a moment longer in the holy Apostolic line. That line in all ages is made up of those who "are built on the foundation of the Apostles and Prophets, Jesus Christ himself being the chief corner-stone." Built on them in what manner? By regular ordination from the Apostles? If so, the Man of Sin is the minister of God, and the Mother of Abominations is the spouse of Christ. But this cannot be. That glorious and holy line runs through all ages, composed of those who have embraced, gloried in, and preached that blessed Gospel which Prophets predicted, which Apostles unfolded, and of which Christ is the chief corner-stone. Any other descent from the Apostles than this is no better than the descent of the carnal Israel from Abraham. The line of ordination may be as distinct as was the line of descent from Abraham to the Jews in the time of our Lord. But what saith Christ? " If ye were Abraham's children, ye would do the works of Abraham." But " ye are of your father the devil, and the works of your father ye will do." And so now, show us a man who perverts the Gospel, who preaches another Gospel which is not another, and let his pretensions to be a successor to the Apostles be what they may, we say the tie in which he glories is outward, carnal, useless. He is no minister of Christ. We appeal to our authority. We claim humble and universal subjection to it ; for it is not the word of man, nor the voice of antiquity, nor of fathers, nor of councils, but the word of the living God. " As we said before, so say I now again, If ANY man preach any other Gospel unto you than that ye have received, let him be ACCURSED." (Gal. i. 9.)

We shall next advert to the *fourth* point, which we have said it was necessary for our Oxford brethren to prove before they could successfully maintain their position—namely, that no power is left to the Church in the event of those who are outwardly ordained, preaching another than the Gospel of Christ to cast them off, and substitute for them the faithful in Christ Jesus.

This world is marred by sin. After the fall, when He who " willeth that all men should be saved and come to the knowledge of the truth," revealed himself to Adam, to Noah, to Abraham, to the Jewish people by Moses, it was for the salvation of themselves and their posterity. But they liked not to retain God in their knowledge ; they forsook him ; and wrath, again and again, has come, and will come, upon all such to the uttermost.

In like manner, Christ having redeemed man and ascended on high, sent his Holy Spirit fully to develop his glorious Gospel to his Church through the medium of the Apostles. While he was on earth, and before the Spirit was given, they could not "bear" (John xvi. 12) nor understand the mystery of the Gospel. It was only after " He, the Spirit of truth, was come" that they were led "into ALL TRUTH," and were directed and enabled, under his plenary inspiration, to unfold it in all its unmeasurable fulness and just proportions, for the use of the Church, till the end of time. Under the direction of the Spirit, they also ordained " faithful men," who should succeed them in preaching the Gospel and dispensing the ordinances of the Christian faith from age to age. As in the former and imperfect revelations of God to his creatures, so in this, had they remained faithful to the trust committed to them, what a blessed age would have been introduced into this sinful world. But we all know this was not the case even in the Apostolic age. Soon those arose in the Church who even denied the Lord that bought them, and brought upon themselves swift destruction. (2 Peter ii. 1.) St. Paul says, in his address to THE ELDERS of Ephesus, " I know this, that after my departing shall grievous wolves enter in among you, not sparing the flock. *Also of your own selves* (among you bishops) shall men arise, speaking perverse things to draw disciples after them." (Acts xx. 30.) And before St. Paul uttered these words, " *the mystery of iniquity*" did already work in the Church, and it ceased not exhibiting itself in innumerable heresies, among all ranks in the Church, till " *that Wicked was fully revealed, whose coming was after the working of Satan, with all power, and signs, and lying wonders, and with all deceivableness of unrighteousness.*" (2 Thes. ii. 9.)

Now, we say, was there no help for the Church in these circumstances? For centuries there appeared none. " The Man of Sin and son of perdition," resting on this same " APOSTOLIC SUCCESSION," wasted the true Church of God, and trampled under foot the saints of the Most High. A poor German monk was at last enlightened by God to see the truth which Rome had hidden from the world, and he had strength given him to break the spell which bound men in the chains of the Mother of Abominations. Previous, indeed, to the Reformation, others, and especially the Waldenses and Albigenses, had characterised Rome aright, and separated themselves from her and " the Apostolic line," as our Oxford brethren understand it. But at the latter glorious era, the Churches of England, Scotland, and Ireland, the German, Swiss, and French Protestant Churches, guided by men whose names will be venerated throughout all time, declared " the holy Catholic Church" to be ANTICHRIST, in terms the most simple and precise. They separated from her as the accursed of God. They cared not for the thunders of her excommunications. And resting on Christ as the chief corner-stone, and building themselves up in the doctrines of the Apostles and Prophets, they established the various Protestant Churches throughout Europe. Different, indeed, were these newly constituted Churches of Christ in outward things,—in ceremonies, traditions, ritual, and in matters non-essential, and this, according to our Church, was quite right, " for at all times they have been divers, and may be changed according to the diversities of countries, time, and men's manners, so that nothing be ordained against God's word." (Article 34.) But they severally rested on Christ. They established a goodly order within their respective boundaries for the ministry of the word, the administration of the Sacraments, the ordination of ministers, and all things necessary for the constitution and healthful operation of the body of Christ. They acknowledged and gloried in one another. We have seen Bishop Hall speaking of different Reformed foreign Churches as " the dear spouse of Christ." We have seen different bishops of the first name in our Church sitting in the Presbyterian Synod of Dort. And we see, in conformity with this catholic spirit, our Church authoritatively decide, in her 19th Article, that " the visible Church of Christ is a congregation of faithful men, in the which the pure word of God is preached, and the Sacraments be duly administered, according to Christ's ordinance in all those things that of necessity are requisite to the same."

We thus see that *in practice* the Fathers of the Reformation dethroned the Man of Sin, who had perverted the Gospel, and replaced him by pastors who should feed the flock of Christ with understanding and knowledge. And if what we have said on the collateral subjects be duly considered—that no passage is to be found in the New Testament forbidding to preach the Gospel even in circumstances which beyond all others seemed to provoke the prohibition; that such passages as Rom. x. 15, 1 Cor. iv. 1, Heb. v. 4, which are often advanced as having this bearing, have only to be read with the context to be seen to be wholly inapplicable; if the self-evident truth be borne in mind that whatever was done outwardly, Christ never ordained a single individual to pervert his Gospel or abuse his Sacraments; when it is kept in view that in the General Epistle of Jude, not only bishops and the clergy, but *the whole company of the Faithful* are exhorted " *earnestly to contend for the faith which was once delivered to the saints*," we cannot doubt that the conduct of the Reformers was wholly in accordance with the word and will of God, in cutting down all the lofty pretensions of the Church of Rome, whether resting on the *Apostolical Succession* or any other assumption professedly of a heavenly or earthly origin; and equally so, in delivering themselves from her deadly embrace, and fixing in their respective communities and " congregations," an order for the ordination of ministers which they deemed most in accordance with the word of God, and most comely and convenient in the very different circumstances in which they severally accomplished their deliverance from the bondage of the Man of Sin. Such as these were the views entertained on the subject by the most distinguished and honoured of the Reformers; and such, we firmly believe, are in accordance with the spirit and precept of the Scriptures, and with the mind and will of Christ;—while they overthrow the doctrine of the *Apostolical Succession,* as held by the Oxford brethren, and trench sensibly on the vicious and dangerous figments which stand in close relation to it.

All that we have advanced on this branch of the subject tends to the establishment of the following truths :—

1. That while a godly order was established in the Apostolical Church, under the command of Christ, for the successive ordination of ministers, that merciful institution of God was gradually rendered of none effect by the introduction of error and heresy, which more and more prevailed,till the Gospel was for the most part perverted and lost.

2. That schism in the Apostolical Church, or in "any congregation of faithful men, in the which the pure word of God is preached, and the Sacraments be duly administered according to Christ's ordinance" (Art. 19), is highly sinful and greatly to be deprecated.

3. That in the nature of things and by the constitution of the Gospel, men who, instead of preaching the Gospel, pervert it, and who, instead of administering the Sacraments, abuse them, though they have been outwardly ordained, have received no ordination from Christ,—on the contrary, they are declared by the Spirit to be " accursed." So that as in the Sacrament of the Supper, they who " be void of a lively faith, although they do carnally and visibly press with their teeth the Sacrament of the body and blood of Christ, yet in nowise are they partakers of Christ, but rather eat and drink to their condemnation" (Art. 29); so the unfaithful bishop or pastor, though carnally and visibly ordained, hath received no authority from Christ, and only perverts the Gospel to his higher condemnation.

4. That to separate from a community of professedly Christian men, " in which the pure word of God is *not* preached, and the Sacraments are *not* duly administered according to Christ's ordinance," is not schism, but is an imperious duty, whether viewed in relation to ourselves or others.

5. That from the whole tenor and scope of the New Testament Scriptures—from no one being forbidden in them to preach the Gospel, even in circumstances which to ordinary reason would have called for the prohibition—from the object of the ordinance of preaching, and the nature of the Sacraments—it may be concluded, that where a part of the body of Christ has *justly* and *rightly* separated themselves on account of heresy from a professedly Christian Church, they have authority from Christ to call to the ministry pastors who have knowledge and faith to lead them in the path of life; that to this view the most distinguished of the Reformers in substance subscribed ; while the blessing of the Great Head of the Church, which

has strikingly rested on bodies so constituted, confirms the accuracy of the views to this effect, which have been drawn immediately from the fountain of Truth.

Lastly. That the attempt of the Oxford brethren to rest the safety of the Church upon " *the Apostolical Succession*," transmitted to them through a long succession of men, who, though visibly and carnally ordained, were never called or ordained by Christ, but who, as perverters of his Gospel and abusers of his Sacraments, He declares to be *accursed*, is a fond and vain thing, discountenanced by the Articles of our Church, repudiated by the most distinguished Reformers, and strikingly repugnant to the Word of God.

CHAPTER III.

BAPTISMAL REGENERATION.

MANY of our readers may be disposed to think, even from the slight specimens which we gave in the last chapter of the dogmas of the High Church party, that they so palpably rise from the same ground as Popery, and are so identical with it in principle and aim, that few indeed will be taken with a hook so clumsily baited. But if, on the other hand, there be brought into view the character, station, and influence of some of those by whom these principles are disseminated; that they are men of the first literary and official rank in the University, and accordingly possess over multitudes of the younger clergy, now scattered through the country, that peculiarly strong influence which the relative situation of tutor and pupil generally engenders and perpetuates; when we remember that the author of the *Christian Year* is of the number of these instructors, and that the softness and elegancies of poetry are thus brought in aid of the dignity of learning and the early associations of university life, we see little reason for surprise at the measure of success with which the strenuous efforts of these men are accompanied. And this the rather, when it is considered that the work is not hastily prepared: that the tracts are carefully written, and yet skilfully diversified in matter and manner; that there is an extensive combination for the purpose; and that if some writers contribute four pages to the series, Professor Pusey elaborated last year one continuous train, extending to 295 pages of close letter-press. No one who has even a slight acquaintance with the plausible grounds and arguments by which pure Popery is vindicated, would fail to expect an abundant harvest to be reaped by her, if in circumstances so favourable as those at which we have now glanced, she could circulate the vindication of her ruinous doctrines through the country, and especially impress them with such commanding advantage upon the minds of the younger clergy. If so, how much greater may be the effect in the present instance? Assuredly if we know any thing at all of history or of Scripture, we never saw learning, station, and influence more grievously misapplied and perverted. We question not the purity of the intention. We have only to do with the effect.

Our readers perceive distinctly the object of our Oxford brethren. Under existing circumstances, they are desirous of bringing their tribute of support to the Establishment; and this consists in the attempt to call men's attention back to certain properties, which, they say, are peculiar to the English Church, and which are indispensable to the constitution of the true Church. These are the APOSTOLIC SUCCESSION, and the SACRAMENTS *received as the grand appointed means for infusing the divine life into the soul, and preserving it when so infused.* The Church of Scotland, the Continental Churches generally, and, of course, the whole body of Dissenters, have not got the APOSTOLIC SUCCESSION; accordingly they cannot *administer the Sacraments;* and the result is, that all the members of these false Churches and religious communities are without Chirst, or the life which he imparts to his people. The members, in the aggregate, are given over to the uncovenanted mercies of God, and their teachers are involved in the condemnation of Korah, Dathan, and Abiram. The practical improvement to be drawn from this teaching is obvious to the meanest comprehension. It is this:—" Hasten then, all people from these refuges of lies, and find truth and salvation within the bosom of our Apostolical Church." Such also, exactly, is the language of the Romish Apostacy, only she extends her lines, and includes Professor Pusey, the author of the *Christian Year*, the editor of the *British Magazine*, and all their Reverend coadjutors in the condemnation of Korah, and she views the whole English Church as lapsed and excommunicated heretics. The latter rise up with indignation against the sentence of Rome. We protest with sorrow, but with all firmness, against the other equally unscriptural judgment. We should certainly do so, did these errors stand apart and alone, without affecting the integrity of the fundamental principles and doctrines which constitute the way of life opened to mankind by the mission and sacrifice of our Lord: for even in this case they were most lamentable and hurtful. But

when we know that they stand in intimate and inseparable union with
the fundamental doctrines of Christ; that they affect, not only so as
to obscure, but even to destroy them, we feel the necessity laid upon
us to pronounce and to prove that they are opposed to the Word of
God; that they have their origin in that " mystery of iniquity," which,
working in the Apostolic age, issued, as the Holy Ghost teaches us,
in the Romish Apostacy, and which will and must work to similar or
worse ends, at whatever age of the Church it is again permitted to
have free course.

We discussed in the last chapter the subject of the *Apostolical
Succession*. We have shown that the extreme doctrines on this
subject advanced by our Oxford brethren receive no countenance
from the Articles of the Church whose children they profess to be—
that they have no foundation in Scripture—and are negatived by the
remarkable communications of the peculiar graces of the Spirit,
evidenced by their corresponding fruits, which have, and which do
distinguish various of those Churches which they so repudiate and
condemn. A dogma it is, hard indeed to believe, and which would
require to rest on evidence of the most irrefragable description :—
that the Saviour, after directing the glad tidings of salvation to be
published to every creature under heaven, and inviting every human
being to whom the glorious tidings should come to drink to the
full of the waters of life, should have contracted the channels, (how
or when no one can tell,) so that none should drink of it unless
administered by men who had themselves defiled and then sealed
up the fountain of living waters, or by those who derived their
authority to dispense them immediately from those who had thus
frustrated the grace of God, and were in consequence lying under his
recorded curse and condemnation! It is acknowledged, that for
centuries, to speak generally, the Pope, the bishops, and the priests
of the Romish community did " not preach the Gospel, but another
Gospel, which is not another;" and, consequently, that they lay under
the curse of God. (Gal. i. 3, 9.) It will be acknowledged that,
though they received the form of ordination from men, they were
never ordained by God. The words were said to them, " Receive ye
the Holy Ghost; whosesoever sins ye remit, they are remitted, and
whosesoever sins ye retain, they are retained;" but they were never
said to them by God. They never received the Holy Ghost as the
ministers of Christ. They remitted sins constantly which were never
remitted of Heaven, and retained those which were blotted out in the
blood of the Lamb. In fact, they had no part nor lot in this ministry,
into which they were thrust, or had thrust themselves, but were the
tools of Satan, instead of being the shepherds and bishops of souls.

Were these men ever called to the ministry by the Holy Ghost?
Never. Could these priests of the synagogue of Satan be, not only
a medium, but the only medium by which the Holy Ghost was
conveyed to his Church in future ages? This is the assertion. It is
one revolting, not only to the feelings of the regenerated heart, but
opposed to all experience, and to the whole spirit and tone of Scripture, and though authority for the dogma may be found in human
tradition, in vain will it be sought for in the word of God.

Having thus said what we deem necessary on the subject of the
Apostolical Succession, the Sacrament of BAPTISM, as received by our
Oxford brethren, is that which next falls to be considered; this of
course involves the question of BAPTISMAL REGENERATION.

It is the first requisite to the satisfactory examination of this
part of the subject to understand the views taken of it by our Oxford
friends. The importance of this part of the question they perceive
to be very great, and accordingly, as we have already hinted,
Professor Pusey has dedicated 295 pages to the illustration of it. As
this Reverend Dignitary may be considered to be the head and leader
of the confederacy, it is satisfactory to have his own statements to
submit to our readers, as those likely to be most accurate, and most
in unison with the principles of the entire body. With this object in
view, we make the following extracts, which are exclusively from the
writings of Professor Pusey.

"By Baptism, our blessed Saviour tells us, we are born again:
Baptism is, God tells us by his apostle, the washing of regeneration,
and the renewal by the Holy Ghost; through it, we are incorporated
into Christ, made members of his body, engraffed into Him, made
partakers of his death, burial, and resurrection: by it, through His
merits, the original taint of our nature was forgiven, and our old man
crucified. We ourselves have put on Christ, and so become partakers
of the Sonship of the ever-blessed Son of God. 'By it we are saved;'
i. e., for the time actually saved (as one may know in the case of
baptized infants), and subsequently, in a state of actual salvation,
(not merely of capacity of salvation), unless we fall from it: through
it we are anointed by God's Holy Spirit, sealed by Him, and have
the first earnest of our future inheritance given to us. God does not
set forth Baptism merely as the introduction into the Christian
covenant, and so entitling the baptized person hereafter to Christian
privileges; but as putting him already in possession of them in part,
as a pledge of their fuller enjoyment of those which are capable of
increase; i. e., those which the recipient afterwards becomes capable
of receiving in fuller abundance. It was but to be expected, that
these privileges being thus great, the loss of them should be, in
proportion, dreadful; and that there being, as St. Chrysostom says,
no second, third, or fourth Baptism, the loss should be as a whole,
irreparable. Such is the view which all Christian antiquity took of
the warnings of St. Paul; nor does any other meaning appear so

probable, as neither have we now such good means of deciding the question, as those who yet spoke St. Paul's language, and lived nearer to his times." *

" Not, manifestly, as if the faith and longing desires, and yearnings, and prayers of the parents for the child were of no benefit to it, or again, that the prayers of the congregation, which the Church solicits for each infant, availed nothing ; but only, that no faith, or desires, or prayers, or anything besides, were of such moment as *to affect* the virtue which Christ has annexed to His sacrament of Baptism, or, as if the regeneration of our infants were to be ascribed in any way to our prayers instead of Christ's ordinance. Larger measures of grace He, doubtless may bestow in answer to more fervent prayers ; and it would argue a sinful want of sympathy, were the Church not to pray, when God is about, by her means, to engraff a new member into the body of His Son ; and, therefore, we pray ; but not as if God's mercy was so limited to our prayers, that He would not render Christ's ordinance effectual to one *who opposed it not*, although we sinned in our mode of administering it." †

" It is not, then, on account of any intrinsic holiness of the parents, or any faith inherent in them, but of ' God's abundant mercy,' that He hath called us ; having committed to his Church the power of administering His sacraments, and annexing to her exercise of faith in so doing, the blessing of His sacrament, where there is no opposing will, and accordingly to us, whom He called before we had done either good or evil." ‡

" In adults, faith was required, but only as removing an obstacle to the beneficial workings of God's Spirit through the sacraments." §

" ' Let no one tell me,' says St. Bernard, ' that an infant has not faith, to whom the Church imparts her's. Great is the faith of the Church.' " ‖

" Let us hear St. Gregory of Nazianzum commending Infant Baptism. ' Hast thou an infant ? Let not wickedness gain an opportunity against it. Let it be sanctified from a babe. Let it be hallowed by the Spirit from its tenderest infancy. Fearest thou the seal of faith, on account of the weakness of nature, as a faint-hearted mother, and of little faith ? . . . Thou hast no need of Amulets— IMPART TO HIM THE TRINITY, that great and excellent preservative.' The thrill which those impressive words, ' Impart to him the Trinity, (δὸς αὐτῷ τὴν Τριάδα) echoing to us after 1,400 years, still awaken in us, may well make us admire the energy of the faith, which infused into words so simple, a force so amazing. The words are nothing : the fact is the ordinary privilege of Christians ; but the faith in the power of God, as manifested in the Baptism of every infant brought to Him, the realizing of those privileges, as implied in those words, overwhelms us, because our faith has not been equal to it." ¶

" ' This illumination (Baptism) then,' says St. Gregory of Nazianzum, ' is the brightness of souls, the transformation of life, the interrogatory of conscience towards God ; it is the help of our weakness, putting off of the flesh, following of the Spirit, participation

* *Tracts for the Times*, vol. ii., page 196.   † Ibid., page 158.
‡ Ibid., p. 164.   § Ibid., p. 129.   ‖ Ibid., p. 154.   ¶ Ibid., p. 173.

of the Word, restoration of our nature, the flood which drowneth sin, communication of light, dissipation of darkness. The "illumination," is a chariot up to God, an absence with Christ, a staff of faith, a perfecting of the mind, a key of the kingdom of heaven, the exchange of life, the destruction of bondage, the loosing of chains . . . we call it gift, grace, baptism, anointing, enlightening, garment of immortality, washing of regeneration, seal, and every other name of honour—gift, as being given to us who had nothing to offer—grace, as being debtors—dipping, in that sin was buried with us in the water—anointing, as being sacred and royal, for such are men wont to anoint—enlightening, as being brightness itself—garment, as a covering of shame—washing, as a cleansing—seal, as keeping us, and an emblem of dominion. In this do the heavens rejoice, this do the angels magnify, for its kindred brightness: this is an image of the blessedness yonder; this we would gladly praise in hymns, but cannot as we would.'

"These are indeed fervid words and thoughts that burn; yet are they also words of truth and soberness; words, which because they are glowing, approach the nearer to the truth; and are sober, because expressive of reality. It is not the language of declamation, but of a soul, which having now been 'carried to hoar hairs,' would fain express the greatness of God's benefits, but 'cannot, as it would.'" *

These sentiments no one can mistake, and accordingly we present them to our readers without a single comment, as the basis on which will rest many of our future remarks.

The next question is, On what authority do our Oxford brethren profess to rest these theological opinions? We reply, on three authorities; and were they indeed fixed on the triple basis on which they profess to rest them, no power could overthrow their positions. They professedly rest them on *Scripture*, on the *Articles of our Church* and on the *judgment of the whole Church* before corrupted by Popish errors. We shall find in the progress of our investigation that *Scripture* will not sustain them; that *our own Church* will not uphold them; and, finally, we shall examine, and test the value of, the opinions on the subject of the early Fathers of the Church, on which the Oxford divines are disposed to rest with peculiar complacency, and to build with unhesitating confidence. We shall refer to these alleged authorities in the order we have named.

To refer, then, in the *first* place, to Scriptural authority, we have just seen the view of this holy ordinance received by our Oxford brethren. It may be convenient, with a view to distinctness, to take from other, and higher authority, a statement of what we may really expect to find in Scripture on the subject of Christian baptism.

Our own Church states, in her 27th Article, that—

"Baptism is not only a *sign* of profession, and mark of difference,

---

* *Tracts for the Times*, vol. ii., page 181.

whereby Christian men are discerned from others that be not
christened, but it is also a SIGN of regeneration or new birth,
whereby, as by an instrument, they that receive Baptism rightly are
grafted into the Church; the promises of forgiveness of sin, and
of our adoption to be the sons of God by the Holy Ghost, are visibly
signed and sealed; faith is confirmed, and grace increased by virtue
of prayer unto God. The Baptism of young children is in any wise
to be retained in the Church, as most agreeable with the institution
of Christ."

The Church of Scotland states in her Catechism that " Baptism is
a Sacrament wherein the washing with water in the name of the
Father, the Son, and the Holy Ghost, doth signify and seal our
engrafting into Christ, and partaking of the benefit of the covenant of
grace and our engagement to be the Lord's."

Calvin, as quoted by Pusey, states, that a Sacrament "is an
outward symbol whereby the Lord seals to our consciences the
promises of his good will towards us, to sustain the weakness of our
faith; and we, on the other hand, attest our piety before Him, angels,
and men."

It must be acknowledged by all, that while there is a striking
harmony subsisting in these three definitions of Baptism, they are all
very far removed from the views of the Sacrament afforded by the
extracts which we have given from the writings of our Oxford
brethren; and a very simple reference to Scripture will assuredly
and speedily discover which makes the nearest approximation to
Divine truth.

The subject, if we mistake not, is very much clouded and embar-
rassed by blending parts of it together, which, in many important
points of view, are distinct, namely *adult* and *infant* Baptism. We
shall keep them distinct, and treat, in the first instance, of *adult*
Baptism.

Water Baptism, as is well known, was common among the Jews.
John came "baptizing with water" and "preaching the Baptism of
repentance for the remission of sins." During the personal ministry
of our Lord, Baptism was administered to those who professed to be
his disciples (" though Jesus himself baptized not, but his disciples");
and the same rite was solemnly directed by our Lord, in giving his
commission to his Apostles to preach the Gospel, immediately
previous to his ascending to heaven, to be administered to all his
professed disciples throughout all ages. St. John does not record the
commission. St. Luke records the command to preach the Gospel,
but not to administer Baptism, in the following words :—" Thus it is
written, and thus it behoved Christ to suffer, and to rise from the

dead on the third day: and that repentance and remission of sins should be preached in his name among all nations, beginning at Jerusalem. And ye are witnesses of these things." The entire commission is recorded both by St. Matthew and St. Mark. The words of the latter are these—"Go ye into all the world and preach the Gospel to every creature; he that believeth and is baptized shall be saved; but he that believeth not shall be damned." So far, then, we have no hint or appearance of the identification of the thing signified, with "the sign."

Let us now refer to "the acts of the Apostles" in obedience to the Divine commission which they had received. In every case it will be found there was first the profession of faith, and then the administration of the ordinance. There was first *faith*, "*the New Birth*," then "*the sign of regeneration*," and "*of profession*," affixed upon the convert, in accordance with the institution and command of our Lord. The whole may be seen distinctly from one example, that of the eunuch and Philip. "Here is water," said he, "what doth hinder me to be baptized? and Philip said, *If thou* BELIEVEST *with all thine heart*, thou mayest." A degree of obscurity is frequently introduced into the subject, from the effusion of the *miraculous gifts* of the Spirit which in those days accompanied or followed faith and the administration of the Sacrament. But these ought to be put out of sight when viewing the subject at present in hand. That they were miraculous gifts which ceased with, or shortly after, the Apostolic age is admitted, and is obvious from the fact that they were outwardly manifest both to Peter and those who accompanied him to Cornelius, as well as to the outward senses of Simon Magus, and, indeed, of all who witnessed them.

Our Oxford brethren indeed controvert the above representation, and Professor Pusey considers that the case of St. Paul furnishes an example of the truth of their views of Baptismal Regeneration. He says, " before his Baptism he appears neither to have been pardoned, regenerated, justified, nor enlightened." " But as yet," he continues, (that is, previous to his Baptism,) " neither were his sins forgiven, nor had he received the Holy Ghost, and consequently was not born again of the Spirit *before it was conveyed to him through his Saviour's Sacrament*." " But, if even to St. Paul," continues professor Pusey, " for whose conversion our Saviour himself vouchsafed again to become visible to human sight, Regeneration and the other gifts of the Holy Spirit were not imparted without the appointed Sacrament of grace, why should this be expected or looked for by others? (*Tracts for the Times*, vol. ii., pp. 47, 48.)

Let us consider the simple circumstances of the case. Saul, the persecutor, was on his way to Damascus, "*breathing out threatenings and slaughter* against the disciples of the Lord." The Lord appeared unto him, and His glory struck him to the ground. He informed him, in reply to his inquiry, "Who art thou, Lord?" "I am Jesus whom thou persecutest:" and added, "it is hard for thee to kick against the pricks. But rise and stand upon thy feet: for I have appeared unto thee for this purpose, to make thee a minister and a witness both of those things which thou hast seen, and of those things in the which I will appear unto thee." (Acts ix. 5, and xxvi. 15.) The response was, "Lord, what wilt thou have me to do?" Here, by the mighty power of God was the lion changed into the lamb. The man who the moment before was "breathing out slaughter" against the Lord, is sitting at his feet, being instructed by Christ himself that he was to be "the minister and witness" of the truth. In the wisdom of God, however, Paul, like most other true converts, remained, not merely naturally blind, but probably suffering under conviction of sin, and in the pangs of sorrow and repentance for three days. "He was three days with-sight, and neither did eat nor drink." For the perfecting of his work, it pleased God to resort to the usual means. "And Ananias went his way, and entered into the house; and putting his hands on him said, Brother Saul, the Lord, even Jesus, that appeared unto thee in the way as thou camest, hath sent me that thou mightest receive thy sight, and be filled with the Holy Ghost. And *immediately* there fell from his eyes as it had been scales, and he received sight forthwith, and arose and was baptized. And when he had received meat, he was strengthened." (Acts ix. 17.) The removal of his natural blindness was no doubt accompanied by the removal of whatever darkness still brooded over his spirit, and probably at the same moment the Holy Ghost, in all his miraculous as well as enlightening influences, rested upon him in abundant measure. Ananias says, "that thou mightest receive thy sight, and be filled with the Holy Ghost." "*Immediately*," it is recorded, the one took place, clearly intimating the impartation of the other.

In opposition, then, to Professor Pusey we say, "that Regeneration and the gifts (and graces) of the Holy Spirit were imparted *previous* to the appointed Sacrament of Grace." After he was baptized, the only further statement made, is, that "when he had received meat, he was strengthened." But what proofs of conversion and regeneration have we before Baptism was administered? A change of heart, of affections, of will—a humble inquiry of Him whom he was perse-

cuting, " what wouldest thou have me to do?" Prayer, "for behold
he prayeth,"—obviously true, spiritual, acceptable *prayer*, for that he
had previously constantly prayed as a self-righteous Pharisee, is beyond a question. And the intimation given to himself, in which he
wholly acquiesced, that he was to be made " a minister and witness "
to that despised faith which to that moment he sought to destroy. Yet
this man, so circumstanced, was, according to Professor Pusey, " neither
pardoned, regenerated, justified, nor enlightened."

The only semblance of foundation for this opinion, on which Professor Pusey can take his stand, is the relation of the important
transaction, in Acts xxii. 12, in which the following words of Ananias
are introduced :—" And now, why tarriest thou? arise, and be baptized, and wash away thy sins, calling upon the name of the Lord."
But we think it evident that nothing further from these expressions
can be drawn than this—that Paul not only having afforded evidence
with the eunuch, that he " *believed with all his heart*," but Ananias,
having been assured by the Lord that he was " a chosen vessel unto
Him," exhorted him, as he was a partaker of the heavenly grace, to
become also, according to the commandment of Christ, a partaker of
the sacred ordinance by which " the washing away of his sins, and
his adoption to be the son of God by the Holy Ghost, would be
visibly signed and sealed" (Art. 27.) to his heart and conscience, as
well as the indispensable public profession of his faith made. In the case
of the eunuch, Philip consented to his baptism only if he " believed
with all his heart." In no other case can the sign and seal of the
New Birth be rightly and scripturally administered. The faith which
justifies unquestionably existed in Saul of Tarsus before Baptism was
administered, and by the administration of the ordinance his " Faith"
was, no doubt, " confirmed, and grace increased, by virtue of prayer
unto God," (Art. 27,) or, in the words of Ananias, by " calling on the
name of the Lord." We submit that any other reading of the passage
is contrary to the analogy of faith, as well as in opposition to the
Articles of our venerable Establishment; and would to God that all
our Oxford brethren, and all who may read these lines, were changed,
and regenerated, and pardoned, to the extent that Saul was previous
to Ananias laying his hands upon him.

We are sorry that we have been so long detained by this digression;
but as Professor Pusey has somewhat carefully elaborated the case, as
the Bishop of Exeter has written a most erroneous discourse on the
subject, in the series of Sermons published under the patronage of
the Christian Knowledge Society, and as it fairly stood in our
way, we considered ourselves forced to remove it, before leaving

the consideration of the *acts of the Apostles* consequent upon their commission, and proceeding to consider the *direct statements of Scripture* with reference to this interesting subject.

Before we do so, however, we may briefly refer to the conduct of the Apostles with reference to this Sacrament in another point of view. If by Baptism, as Professor Pusey says, we " put on Christ, and so become partakers of the Sonship of the ever-blessed Son of God ;" in short, by it receive everything that God communicates by Christ to his Church, it is undeniable that St. Paul must have been in the last degree desirous to have *baptized* his converts. His zeal to win souls to Christ, we all know was beyond adequate description. His desire to have an innumerable company of those who should be his joy and crown of rejoicing in the day of the Lord, how intense ! How anxious, therefore, must he have been by his own hands to " IMPART TO THEM THE TRINITY !" How do such imaginations fly before the words of the Apostle in the first chapter of the 1st of Corinthians, " *I thank God* that I baptized none of you, but Crispus and Gaius ; lest any should say that I had baptized in mine own name. And I baptized also the household of Stephanus ; besides, *I know not whether I baptized any other*. For Christ sent me not to baptize, but to preach the Gospel." But does the Apostle speak in a manner so careless and indifferent of those who, through his instrumentality, had believed through grace ? Let us mark. To the same Corinthians he says, " for though ye have ten thousand instructors in Christ, yet have ye not many fathers ; *for in Christ Jesus I have begotten you through the Gospel.*" (1 Cor. iv. 15.) Not, let it be observed, through *Baptism*, in regard to which, he is obviously careless whether he administered it to them or not. To the Galatians he says, " My little children, *of whom I travail in birth* again till Christ be formed in you." (Galatians iv. 19.) To Philemon he says, " I will repay it ; albeit I do not say to thee *how thou owest unto me even thine ownself besides.*" (Phil. 19.) More quotations in the way of contrast are uunecessary ; and as St. Paul thus contemplated Baptism, in the like manner did St. Peter. Neither obviously did *he* think that this was the method of " *imparting the Trinity*" to his converts. When the Holy Ghost had descended on the household of Cornelius " he *commanded* them to be baptized in the name of the Lord." (Acts x. 48.)

A most amiable friend of ours, entertaining the High Church principles which we combat, has suggested to us that Saint Paul thus slightly speaks of Baptism (comparatively) because the administration of it did not belong to the Apostolic office. But this idea is dissipated by St. Paul's own words. He contrasts the administration of Baptism, not with any peculiar duty of the Apostolic office, but with the great work of the other faithful servants of Jesus Christ in all ages, namely, the preaching of the Gospel. "Christ sent me not to *baptise*, but to PREACH THE GOSPEL." Was *the less* charge given to the Apostle and *the greater* to the ordinary ministers of the word? His supreme delight was to "impart the Trinity" to his hearers, but he expected to do so by the foolishness of preaching, by the impartation to them of that Gospel of which he was made a minister.

In now proceeding to open the next branch of our subject, we may with propriety ask Professor Pusey how he interprets the following text in conformity with his theory? It is by *Baptism*, he says, that we receive the Holy Ghost, and are made partakers of Christ. The Apostle, in the second verse of the third chapter to the Galatians says to that Church, "This only would I learn of you, *received ye the Spirit* by the works of the law, or by the *hearing of faith?*" The Rev. Professor would, according to his principles, reply, "By neither: they received it of course by *Baptism*." In these few words, however, is the important question answered. By no outward rite, or sacrament, is the Spirit, is Christ, is God, received by man:—but BY FAITH.

Let us take another isolated text, and frame from it the most simple syllogism on the Rev. Gentleman's hypothesis. "Whosoever is born of God, overcometh the world." Every baptized child is "born of God." Every baptized child "overcometh the world!"

"With THE HEART man *believeth* unto righteousness, and with the mouth *confession* is made unto salvation." Therefore, "if thou shalt *confess* with thy mouth the Lord Jesus, and shalt *believe in thine heart* that God hath raised him from the dead, thou shalt be saved." "For the Scripture saith, *whosoever believeth on him shall not be ashamed.*" From an extract which was given in the *Record* newspaper from Professor Pusey, in a review of Mr. Dodsworth's Tracts (which may be had of Seeley or Nisbet) it appeared that the Professor had strung a few texts together, which to the ear sounded as if the Scripture said literally that Baptism saved us, while men, in opposition to Scripture, said it *did not*. The *Record* gave, in our judgment, a sufficient insight into the scriptural method of interpreting those *few* texts in accordance with the analogy of faith. They are but few; and in the exercise of the same just method must various other texts be interpreted, whether they relate to St. Peter's alleged supremacy, or to the real presence, or to other heretical or erroneous dogmas, by whomsoever advanced. As much *semblance* of Scriptural authority is offered by most teachers of error in support of their various departures from truth. Of course, as it

respects those three texts last quoted, the same style of remark as the
Professor had recourse to in regard to his opponents might be trans-
ferred to himself.   But what are three, or six texts of this description
in comparison of the immense number in the Bible in which SALVA-
TION is attached to FAITH ALONE, and in respect of which, by such
a process as he resorted to, and Mr. Dodsworth adopted, he might be
made, not indeed apparently, as in the texts he quoted, but in reality,
to limit and deny the word and grace of the Gospel?   "He that
believeth on me hath everlasting life."   (John vi. 47.)   "He that
cometh to me shall never hunger; and he that *believeth* on me shall
never thirst."   (John vi. 35.)   "He that *believeth* on me, though he
were dead, yet shall he live."   (John xi. 25.)   "Whosoever liveth
and *believeth* in me shall never die."   (John xi. 26.)   " The Gospel
is the power of God unto salvation to every one that *believeth.*"
(Rom. i. 16.)   "Christ is the end of the law to every one that *believeth.*"   (Rom. x. 4.)   "He that *believeth* on the Son of God *hath
life.*"   (1 John v. 10.)   "Ye are saved unless ye have *believed* in
vain."   (1 Cor. xv. 2.)   " *Ye believe not* because ye are not of my
sheep."   (John x. 26.)   " *Believe* on the Lord Jesus Christ, and thou
shalt be saved."   (Acts xvi. 31.)   " It pleased God by the foolishness of preaching to save them that *believe.*"   (1 Cor. i. 21.)   "Who
are sanctified by *faith* that is in me."   (Acts xxvi. 18.)   " Ye are
the children of God by *faith* in Christ Jesus." (Gal. iii. 26.)   "That
Christ may dwell in your hearts by *faith.*"   (Eph. iii. 17.)   " Might
receive the promise of the Spirit through *faith.*" (Gal. iii. 8.)   "For by
grace are ye saved through *faith.*"   (Eph. ii. 8.)   But we should exceed
all bounds were we to quote all the texts to this effect in the Scripture.
Let any one, not adequately acquainted with the subject, take up
Cruden's Concordance, and refer merely to the two words *faith* and
believe, and he will be astonished with the vast number of texts which
attribute salvation and all its blessings simply to *faith*—to *belief,*
without a single reference to Baptism, or any other rite, or grace, or
qualification.   And how is this?   " Because," as our Saviour teaches
us, " this is the work of God that ye BELIEVE on him whom he hath
sent."   Till we *believe* in Christ, and so are united to him (and we
can be united to him in no other way but by *faith*) we are nothing,
and can do nothing.   Becoming " one with him" by *faith,* we have
in virtue of that union, " our fruit unto holiness, and the end everlasting life."

Our Oxford brethren see not how, by this teaching of theirs, they
limit the Holy One of Israel, and shut up, in a degree, the mercies of
God from mankind.   Through the sacrifice of Christ, God now offers

salvation, with all its treasures for time and eternity, freely to every creature under heaven to whom the Gospel comes. Our *Lord* says— "*He that cometh unto me, I will* IN NO WISE *cast out.*" The *Spirit* saith, "*And* WHOSOEVER WILL, *let him take of the water of life freely.*" There is nothing wanting on the side of God. And all that is required on the part of man is that which, according to *the constitution of things,* is indispensable; namely, that he should be convinced of his great necessity, and believe in the power and willingness of God, as revealed in Christ, to save him to the uttermost. He has, indeed, in the general course of God's dispensations, to be deeply exercised and tried in many ways, so as to be made *meet* for that heavenly inheritance for which the death and righteousness of Christ constitute his title. But from Him who is his head, he receives the disposition and the ability to "fulfil all righteousness," and by the instrumentality of the Sacraments, and the other appointed means of grace, he grows up into Christ in all things, till he is removed from the imperfect and shadowy services on earth, to the immediate fruition of his Saviour in heaven.

The principles of our Oxford brethren, indeed, as expounded by Professor Pusey, would not only lead to the conclusion that such views as these were false, but they contradict, in terms the most absolute, the great fundamental truth of Scripture to which we have just adverted, and which is presented to mankind in every variety of phraseology which the strength, flexibility, and expansion of language can command, in order to fix indelibly the grand leading truth upon the mind, "*that we are justified by faith only.*" (Article 11.) The views of Professor Pusey on this subject, to which we shall now advert are, indeed, so anti-church, as well as anti-scriptural, that we cannot but marvel at them exceedingly.

The learned Professor says,* "Faith and repentance, in adults, are necessary to the New Birth, *but they are not the New Birth.* That God imparteth, as it pleaseth Him, according to the depths of his wisdom: *it depended not, as faith and repentance in some measure, may, upon the will of man,* but on God, who calleth into his Church whom he will." At page 135 he states that neither Noah, nor any of the saints of God, previous to the coming of Christ, were regenerate; they were sanctified, but not regenerate.

Professor Pusey states above, that faith and repentance in some measure may depend upon the will of man. In opposition to this assertion, however qualified, the Church says in the tenth Article, "The condition of man after the fall of Adam is such, that he cannot turn

---

* *Tracts for the Times,* p. 141.

and prepare himself, by his own natural strength and good works, to FAITH, and calling upon God.' The learned Professor says, such is his condition that he can turn and prepare himself, at least, "in a measure."

But this erroneous assertion, opposed as it is to the Articles of the Church and to Scripture, is not so wonderful and astounding as the other proposition, that a man may have faith and repentance, and yet not possess Regeneration and the New Birth. But what saith the Scripture? "He that *believeth* on me *hath* everlasting life." Can a man have everlasting life without being regenerated and born from above? Professor Pusey says, Yes.—"He that *believeth* on me, though he were dead, yet shall he live." Can this be asserted of an unregenerate person? Professor Pusey says, Yes.—"That ye might receive the promise of the Spirit through *faith*." Can a person receive the Spirit without being regenerate? Professor Pusey says, Yes. One thing, however, the learned Professor is fully convinced of, namely, that the state of Regeneration, or the New Birth, stands in indissoluble union with the state of "sons of God," and he without reserve asserts that the saints of the ancient Church were not the sons of God. But in the sixth chapter of Genesis, at the second verse, this appellation, "the sons of God" is expressly given to them; while it is said in one of the texts quoted above, "Ye *are* THE CHILDREN OF GOD *by faith*," not by *Baptism*. Again, in Rom. viii. 14, it is stated in terms the most absolute, that "as many as are led by the Spirit of God are *the sons of God*." Were the ancient saints not led by the Spirit of God? Again, in John i. 12, it is said, that "to as many as *believed* in his name, he gave power to become *the sons of God*." Did Abraham not believe in the Saviour when he saw his day afar off and was glad? Or did Moses not so believe when he esteemed the reproach of Christ greater riches than the treasures of Egypt? And in what way was any saint in the Patriarchal or Jewish Churches saved, but by *believing* in the Saviour that was to come, "not having received the promises, but having seen them afar off, and embraced them?" And indeed, from John xx. 29, it would appear that their faith carried the privileges of SONSHIP along with it, with the *highest blessing*. "Jesus said unto him, Thomas, because thou hast seen me, thou hast believed: blessed are they that have not seen, and yet have believed."

The faith of the whole Church, from Adam to her latest members, is in substance and essence ONE. In every case it is the gift of God. In every case it rests on Christ as its foundation and object. In every case it is indissolubly connected with the privilege of being

" the sons of God," "which were born, not of blood, nor of the will of the flesh, nor of the will of man, but of God." They are all, without exception, regenerate and new creatures in Jesus Christ,—in the " Lamb of God slain from the foundation of the world."

But these obvious and glorious scriptural truths cannot be made to fit in with the theory that the New Birth is communicated to the soul only in Baptism, and therefore if this is to be held, that must be rejected. "Regeneration or the New Birth," says Professor Pusey, "is a privilege of the Church of Christ; and we dare not extend it where His word doth not warrant us. To the Church alone in this life it belongs to be THE MOTHER *of the sons of God*."* Accordingly, were it be conceded by the Oxford divines that the saving faith of the saints of the Patriarchal and Jewish Churches entitled them to be called " the sons of God," it would follow that Regeneration did originate otherwise than in water Baptism: nay, it would inevitably follow, that even under the Gospel dispensation, Regeneration obviously stood distinct from Baptism,—for, to take the example already particularly referred to, when the eunuch asked if he might be baptized, the response of Philip was, " IF thou *believest with all thine heart*, thou mayest." The Oxford divines must distinguish, therefore, between the true faith of God's elect and Regeneration, otherwise their whole theory falls to the ground. How this distinction is vindicated and supported by the word of God, we leave our readers to decide without a single additional observation.

We now come, as it regards *adult* Baptism, to the second authority, relied upon by our Oxford brethren, namely, that of our venerable Establishment.

Let our readers mark the terms in which our Oxford brethren speak of this Sacrament in the extracts given at the commencement of this Chapter, and the terms of the 27th Article of our Church as also inserted. In the former, Baptism was described, as " the brightness of souls, the transformation of life, the restoration of our nature, the flood which drowneth sin, the communication of light, the dissipation of darkness, a chariot up to God, an absence with Christ, a perfecting of the mind, a key of the kingdom of heaven. " It is a " gift, grace, anointing, enlightening garment of immortality," &c. &c. " In this do the heavens rejoice, this do the angels magnify, for its kindred brightness: this is an image of the blessedness yonder." And these descriptions of Baptism, are stated by Professor Pusey to be given in the words "of truth and soberness," " which, because they are

---

* *Tracts for the Times,* p. 137.

glowing, approach the nearer to the truth." However this may be, assuredly our Church has little sympathy on the subject either with Gregory Nazienzen or with the Reverend Canon of Christ Church.

"Baptism," says our Church, "is not only a *sign* of profession and mark of difference"—what more is it, then? "It is also a SIGN of *Regeneration*, or *New Birth*, whereby, as by an instrument, they that receive Baptism rightly, are grafted into the Church, the promises of forgiveness of sin, and of our adoption to be the sons of God by the Holy Ghost, are *visibly* SIGNED and SEALED; *faith* is *confirmed*, and *grace increased*, by *virtue of prayer unto God*."

The definition is too clear to be made clearer by any remarks of ours: and we wish every man of competent understanding and of candid and unprejudiced mind, only to contemplate these two statements, and say whether the difference between the two is not wholly prodigious and perfectly irreconcileable. That men who almost assume the honour of being exclusively, or at least pre-eminently, the true orthodox sons of the Church, should thus insult her to her face, is a striking sign of the times. And this the more remarkably appears, when it is considered that we have not quoted these words from some occasional formulary of the Church, but that it is her authoritative, formal, deliberate judgment, and as such is placed by her among "the ARTICLES OF RELIGION," to be received and pondered with peculiar reverence by all her members.

In the above Article, it is obvious that *Baptism* is stated merely to be a SIGN of Regeneration or New Birth. In the twenty-fifth Article, the Sacraments generally are stated to be a means of quickening, strengthening, and confirming our faith in Christ :— "Sacraments ordained of Christ be not only badges or tokens of Christian men's profession, but rather they be certain sure witnesses and effectual signs of grace, and God's good will towards us, by the which he doth work invisibly in us, and doth not only quicken, but also strengthen and confirm our faith in him." And in the Catechism, the Sacrament is said to be an "outward and visible *sign* of an inward and spiritual grace, given unto us, ordained by Christ himself, *as a means whereby we receive the same*, and a pledge to assure us thereof." Professor Pusey contrasts this last definition with *Calvin's*, as given at the beginning of this chapter, and says, in Calvin's view THE means whereby we receive the same is excluded."* But by the change of the article, the Professor makes a wonderful change in

---

* *Tracts for the Times*, p. 115.

the meaning and force of the definition given by the Church. It is not according to the Church, "THE *means*," but "A means whereby we receive" the grace of Christ.

To this statement we presume few would object. We are sure we do not. And although the phrase, in the twenty-fifth Article, of "effectual signs," appears to us inferior, in point of simplicity and precision, to the terms of the Article on Baptism, still there is, perhaps, little in the expressions at which even a fastidious person would be disposed to cavil. The Sacraments are, according to this Article, *witnesses* of grace and of God's good will to us. Assuredly they are; and, if witnesses at all, they must be "sure" or true witnesses. But still let it be observed, they are only "*witnesses*" of it. Again the Sacraments are declared to be "*signs*," and "*effectual signs*," of grace. Still, it is to be observed, they are but "signs of it, and are "effectual," for the purposes for which the signs are given, namely, for quickening, strengthening, and confirming our faith in Christ. We conclude, therefore, that this definition of "the Sacraments," as well as those definitions of Baptism which we have quoted from the twenty-seventh Article and the Catechism, stand out in strong contrast and irreclaimable opposition to the extreme and anti-scriptural theories on the subject held by our Oxford brethren.

We find it will be more convenient not to refer to the views and testimony of the Fathers on this part of the subject, till we have also endeavoured to contemplate *infant* Baptism, in the light of Scripture and of our Church; but having thus concluded what we have to say on the subject of *adult* Baptism, we close our observations for the present, by humbly advising these Oxford divines to beware how, with these notions of their's with regard to the *Apostolical Succession*, and the life-giving qualities of the *Sacraments* if administered by priests of the "*Holy Apostolic line* ;"—of their deadness when otherwise dispensed, the consequent deadness of all those to whom they are so administered, and the condemnation of Korah as lying on all those who attempt to dispense them, if they "do not follow them :"—let them beware, we say, that by such teaching they do not attempt to limit the Holy One of Israel—they do not close their eyes while so engaged, against the manifest glorious work of the Spirit of God, as exhibited in the salvation of sinners, and draw down upon themselves, in consequence, the rightful displeasure of the great Head of the Church. When some of them talk of the uncovenanted mercies of God, they show distinctly to every man of competent Christian knowledge, that they know not "what they say, nor whereof they affirm," and moreover, that they need some one to "expound unto them the way of the Lord more perfectly." May wisdom be given to us all " to teach the things which become sound doctrine ;" and having laid the foundation, to take heed how we build thereupon, lest, it being only "wood, hay, and stubble," with which we are busying ourselves, our "work shall be burned," and we, if " saved, yet so as by fire."

CHAPTER IV.

BAPTISMAL REGENERATION.—INFANT BAPTISM.

HAVING considered in the last chapter the doctrine of Baptismal Regeneration in relation to *adult* Baptism, we now proceed to view the dogma as presented to us, and illustrated by *infant* Baptism. Let our readers cheerfully accompany us in this search after *truth*. This inestimable pearl, the labours of our Oxford brethren are calculated to bedim and darken, and to discolour and destroy. O let us be " valiant for THE TRUTH." The passing contentions of the day are worth comparatively nothing. " They come up in a night and perish in a night." But the importance of preserving pure and uncontaminated the truth of God in relation to the salvation of mankind, who shall declare ! And in no way has the devil, in all ages of the Church, been so successful in corrupting and rendering it of noneffect, as by that method denounced by our Lord himself, and now so strikingly exhibited to us, namely, by " teaching for *doctrines* the *commandments of men*." We anew say, and let every faithful servant of his Lord repeat the truth, " To the law and to the testimony: if they speak not according to this word, it is because there is no light in them."

Let us first recur to the *doctrine* as held by our Oxford brethren.

They maintain, in a manner the most absolute and unrestricted, that all infants baptized by a clergyman having the Apostolic commission (as they understand it), and whether or not there be faith in him who administers the ordinance, or in them who are sponsors for the infant, are " born of God." They become, the moment the Sacrament is administered to them, more strictly and in a higher sense, regenerate than were " Noah, Daniel, and Job." " They are the sons of God, which were born, not of blood, nor of the will of the flesh, nor of the will of man, but of God." This is the doctrine.

Let us next glance at some of the consequences of it.

The boldness and force of the Scriptural statements and images by which the condition of man, by nature, is contrasted with his state by grace, is very remarkable, and worthy of all consideration. In his *unregenerate* state, he is *natural, fleshly, uncircumcised, asleep, dead.* "The *natural* man receiveth not the things of the Spirit of God; for they are foolishness unto him; neither *can he know them*, because they are spiritually discerned." (1 Cor. ii. 14.) "They that are in the *flesh cannot* please God." (Rom. viii. 8.) Ye stiffnecked and *uncircumcised* in heart and ears, ye do always resist the Holy Ghost; as your fathers did, so do ye." (Acts vii. 51.) "Awake, thou that sleepest, and arise from the *dead*, and Christ shall give thee life." (Eph. v. 14.) "And you being *dead* in your sins, and the *uncircumcision* of your flesh, hath he *quickened* together with him, having forgiven you all trespasses." (Col. ii. 13.) "And you hath he quickened who were *dead* in trespasses and sins." (Eph. ii. 8.)—In his *regenerate* state, again, man is in a condition the very reverse of this. He is "*spiritual,*" he "lives after the Spirit," he is "circumcised in heart and mind," he is "awake from the snare of the devil," he is "*alive* from the dead." He is born again—born from above. He is the son of God; the heir of God, and the joint heir with Christ. He has received the Spirit of adoption, whereby he cries, Abba, Father. He is the habitation of God through the Spirit. He is the temple of the Holy Ghost. His life is hid with Christ in God; and when Christ, who is his life, shall appear, he also shall appear with him in glory. The whole company of the regenerate are "beloved of God, called to be saints," sanctified in Christ Jesus," "the faithful in Christ Jesus," they "are *in* God the Father, and *in* the Lord Jesus Christ." "They are united to Christ as the branch is to the vine, as the members of the body to the head;" "for we are members of his body, of his flesh, and of his bones."

It must be acknowledged by all that it were impossible to describe the distinction between those that are "in the flesh" and those that are "in the Spirit" in terms more bold, and we had almost said exaggerated, than by those we have now used; and *they* (very different from the rhapsody of Gregory Nazienzen, quoted by Professor Pusey in the last chapter) are, in reality, the "words of truth and soberness," for they are the words of the Spirit of God.

Every child, then, according to our Oxford brethren, who is baptized in the Church of England, or by the priests of apostate Rome ("for the Sacraments be *effectual* because of Christ's institution and promise, although they be ministered by evil men"—26th Article), is "spiritual" is "circumcised in heart and mind," is "alive from the dead," is " the son of God," " the heir of God, and the joint heir with Christ,"· has " received the Spirit of adoption, whereby he cries, Abba, Father," is " sanctified" and " faithful in Christ Jesus," is united to Christ " as the branch is to the vine," and as " the members of the body to the head."

This state and these characteristics, and many others of a similar kind, are asserted in terms the most absolute to belong to all the children of God without exception. The distressing fears and apprehensions which frequently assail many of the regenerate arise from having doubts of their being the children of God. If they were assured they were such, these must be all instantly dissipated; for these and many other statements indissolubly connect them with eternal life; nay, assure all true believers that they already " HAVE eternal life" (John vi. 24), and this additional assurance is given by our Lord himself—" Because I live, ye shall live also." (John xiv. 19.) If, then, in virtue of the New Birth, imparted to every child in Baptism, he is absolutely the child of God, not only these promises, but these characteristics (for they are inseparably connected), invariably distinguish this child of heaven and heir of immortality.

But who that has eyes to see and ears to hear is not pained if not shocked by such representations as these? To a man who knows his Bible, and has been himself the subject of God's renewing grace, they must seem to border on impiety and profaneness. Professor Pusey says it requires *great faith* to believe in such representations. In our apprehension, it requires great ignorance of Scripture united to much genuine Popish feeling and superstition.

All such pretensions to the possession of the Divine Spirit and the Divine life, we are to try by the unerring rule of Scripture; and to say, as is done, that such an inquiry is beyond our province or faculties, is flatly to contradict Scripture. Our Lord says, " Do men gather grapes of thorns, or figs of thistles? Even so every good tree bringeth forth good fruit; but a corrupt tree bringeth forth evil fruit. A good tree cannot bring forth evil fruit, neither can a corrupt tree bring forth good fruit. *Therefore by their fruits ye shall know them.*" (Matt. vii. 16—20.) St. John says, in his first Epistle, chap. iii. verse 10, " In this the children of God are manifest, and the children of the devil: *whosoever doeth not righteousness is not of God.*" And in the 8th verse, " *He that committeth sin is of the devil.*" In chap. viii. of John, at verse 24, our Lord delivers this aphorism, " Whosoever committeth sin is the servant of sin; and at the 47th verse he says, " He that is of God heareth God's words: *ye therefore hear them not, because ye are not of God."* It is unnecessary, as it were easy, to proceed to multiply quotations of this description with the view of proving, from the only infallible standard of truth, that we are called upon and directed to try, *by their fruits,* all such pretensions to be born of God and to have become new creatures in Christ Jesus. In opposition to all such glowing pretensions as those given utterance to by Gregory Nazienzen, and rejoiced over by Professor Pusey, we reply, *" Whosoever doeth not righteousness is* NOT OF GOD." *" He that committeth sin is* OF THE DEVIL."

Look then at the vast masses of baptized Christians in this country, whether in childhood, youth, manhood, or old age, who are either living in open sin, or who, instead of glorying in the cross of Christ, and being united to him as the branch to the vine, are living to the world, to its business, its riches, its honours, or its pleasures.—"THEY ARE NOT OF GOD." In other words THEY ARE NOT THE SONS OF GOD. Observe, it is not we who say so, but God. And so the same is to be asserted, neither more nor less, of the millions of the poor ignorant, befooled, enslaved children of Papal Rome in Ireland and throughout Europe. We do not deny, let it be observed, that there may not be many of these (and we pray God there may be incomparably more than we imagine), who through the guidance of God's Spirit have been led to discern and to lay hold of Christ and of his salvation, amidst all the midnight obscurations in which that apostate community has enveloped the Gospel of the kingdom, and these of course, being born from above, are of the saved ones. But of the rest of these *baptized* Papists who do not discern Christ, who have their trust in other things than in Christ, and whose works are in accordance with their faith :—look to them in Ireland, hoodwinked and degraded by the priesthood; look to them amidst the licentiousness of Italy, the infidelity of France, the besotted ignorance and general moral relaxation of Portugal and Spain, in which countries cargoes of indulgences are still, or were very lately, articles of merchandise; and while you contemplate them, listen to Professor Pusey while he assures you they are the " sons of God, the brethren of Christ, the heirs of God, and joint heirs with Christ."

Is there not in the application of such characteristics, whether to degraded Papists or to nominal and irreligious Protestants, something in the last degree repulsive to the Christian mind? And why so? We reply, not only because the representation is diametrically opposed to the truth of God, but because it is dishonouring to the Saviour, disparaging to the pure nature of his salvation, and to the fruits of his Spirit, which are invariably produced when He regenerates

and takes up his abode in the hearts of men. He frequently conde-
scends, indeed, to visit the vilest, the most degraded, and the most
wicked, while he views the proud and the self-righteous afar off. But
when he does so, it is to raise them from the death of sin to the life of
righteousness—it is to sanctify and to cleanse them—and it is only
when his operations are seen in a change of heart and life that angels
rejoice, and that men may and ought to rejoice with them.

What then do we conclude from these exhibitions of the actual
state of things in the Church and the world, made under the scriptural
direction to "prove all things," but that the state of nominal Christians is diametrically opposed to the character of the "children of
God," as drawn by the Spirit of God; that it clearly and incontestably
exhibits the character of those whom our Lord declares to be " NOT
OF GOD;" that is, "not born of God"—not "the sons of God?" And
this conclusion is reached not illegitimately, or by entering a province
which we have no right to enter, or into a region in which our faculties cannot properly act;—but by pursuing a course which our Lord
himself points out, and which approves itself to the mind, when plainly
laid open, as altogether just, and good, and true.

We hold, then, that these *consequences*, which inevitably follow from
the reception of the doctrine of Baptismal Regeneration, not viewed
and judged of by the carnal eye of sense, but estimated by the word
of God, in strict accordance with the injunction of our Divine Master
directly applicable to the case, prove that it cannot be true. God
gives in his Word certain marks, by which we may ascertain who
"are born of God"—who are "the sons of God." They are distinct,
well defined, written as with a sun-beam. Our Oxford brethren say,
every infant baptized by a man in the Apostolic line is so born of
God, is the son of God. We say it is false, because the marks given
us in Scripture, by which we are directed to ascertain who are "of
GOD," and who are " NOT OF GOD," clearly demonstrate that the
great mass of nominal baptized Christians, whether Protestants or
Papists, whether in childhood, boyhood, manhood, or old age, are destitute of the principles, spirit, and practice, which distinguish the
children of God, while they display lineaments the most distinct of the
character presented to us in Scripture, of men in their natural and
unregenerated condition.

But, of course, our Oxford brethren allege, that they have scriptural
authority for their belief on this subject. We trust we have demon-
strated to the apprehension of every reader of plain and unsophisticated
mind, that, according to Scripture, received in the light in which we
have now contemplated it, they are mistaken. The lights of Scripture

all meet in one centre of truth. Let us endeavour to discover, whether other parts of Scripture which refer to the subject, are in harmony or in opposition to the truths apparently taught by those passages which we have already considered. Our readers will bear in mind, that our attention is now confined to *infant* Baptism.

They, of course, know that, so far from there being any statement in Scripture to the effect that every baptized child is regenerated, there is not a single direction in the New Testament, from beginning to end, directing a child to be baptized. The practice of infant Baptism, however, has appeared to the greatest and best of men of all ages—and especially to the mighty champions of the Reformation— to rest on a sure and solid basis, and this their judgment is confirmed by the appointed "signs following," not on every individual infant baptized, but on the different Churches by whom the practice of Infant Baptism has been practised and vindicated.

The practice is vindicated, first, from its harmony and correspondence with the administration to children of the initiatory rite in the Jewish Church. Next, from different intimations in the New Testament that probably it was administered to children by, or under, the direction of the Apostles. For instance, Lydia "was baptized *and her household.*" (Acts xvi. 15.) St. Paul says—"I baptized also *the household* of Stephanas." (1 Cor. i. 16.) If such passages are taken in connexion with *the fact*, of which no other is better ascertained or more generally admitted, that the practice was universal among the Christians of the early Church, and that no question on the subject was ever opened in the Church for the first fifteen centuries, we have a force of evidence in its favour which must appear irresistible to most minds, and which sufficiently accounts for the general adoption of the practice in the Christian Church.

But while these views prove conclusively, in our judgment, the obligation of the practice of infant Baptism, "as most agreeable with the institution of Christ" (27th Art.), they are laid hold of by the abettors of Baptismal Regeneration as the foundation and support of their system. While, however, the simple statement which we have now made proves them to be abundantly equal to support the practice of *infant Baptism*, the more closely they are examined the more inadequate will they be found to form a foundation for the unscriptural system of *Baptismal Regeneration.*

Let us first advert to the analogy from circumcision. Baptism being substituted for circumcision as the initiatory rite of the Gospel, it is argued that Baptism as much exceeds circumcision in value as the Gospel surpasses the law. We agree to this statement to the extent that as circumcision was valuable in introducing and giving the infant a right to the privileges of the Jewish Church, so is Baptism more valuable, inasmuch as it introduces the infant and gives him a right to the far higher privileges of the Gospel Church. But we deny it, as a wholly false analogy and unjust inference, when it is argued that as circumcision conferred upon the infant the *outward benefits* of the Jewish Church, Baptism confers upon the infant the *inward and spiritual* benefits of the Gospel Church. Those who argue thus, forget that Christ was in the Jewish Church as he is in the Gospel Church: only he was seen by the Jewish saints through the intervention of types and shadows, while to us these have flown away, and he is plainly revealed. Still it is by *faith alone, communicated through grace,* that he was accepted by them, and that he is accepted by us; and to argue fairly from circumcision to Baptism, we must either hold that circumcision conferred merely the outward, or that it conferred both the outward privileges and inward grace which were enjoyed by Abraham, and after him by all his spiritual posterity. If we confine the privilege of circumcision to the outward, but still very important benefits of the Jewish economy, we must limit the privilege of Baptism to the outward, but far higher benefits of the Gospel. And it is only if we include the inward grace which resided in the Jewish Church under circumcision, that we can correctly, according to a just analogy, include the inward grace that is in the Christian Church under Baptism. We presume no one, who knows what argument means, will deny these propositions.

Now, the whole Jewish history shows, and the plain declarations of Scripture prove, that circumcision did not confer the inward grace of Christ. We might quote many texts in confirmation of this assertion: however, we shall content ourselves with one, but it is more than sufficient for the purpose. In the 2d chapter of the Romans, in the 28th and 29th verses, the Apostle says, " For he is not a Jew which is one outwardly; neither is that circumcision which is outward in the flesh; but he is a Jew which is one inwardly; and circumcision is that of the heart, in the spirit, and not in the letter; whose praise is not of men, but of God." We accordingly conclude that as far as the question is dependent upon *the analogy from circumcision,* the supposition of our Oxford friends is negatived that in *infant* Baptism more is conferred than an initiation into the benefit of the inestimably precious privileges of the Gospel. And we also hold that no other conclusion can be legitimately reached from the terms given to both rites in Scripture. Circumcision is called a *sign,* a *seal,* a *covenant.* No higher names are given to Baptism, and it will be perceived that the two first designations are those applied to Baptism by our Church both in the 25th and the 27th Articles (on *the Sacraments* and on *Baptism*).

That the two rites, as administered to infants, are essentially of the same nature, and answer substantially the same ends, may be strongly inferred from the striking similarity of appearance presented by the aggregate members of the two Churches. If, while circumcision simply opened the door to the enjoyment of the privileges of the Jewish Church, we all became, by Baptism, the true spiritual children of God, and this in a higher sense than were Noah, Daniel, and Job, is it not to be expected, as a necessary consequence, that a marked difference would be manifested between the spiritual state of the members of the two Churches? Undoubtedly so. But what is the fact? We perceive the superiority in professing Christians in general, arising from the higher privileges and brighter light of the Gospel dispensation to which those who are baptized are introduced. But beyond this, which is the just and true distinction, we perceive in nominal Christians the same deadness to God, deadness to Christ, and indifference to the things of His kingdom, which distinguished " Israel after the flesh," as contradistinguished from " Israel after the Spirit." It required in the Jewish Church "circumcision of the heart, in the Spirit," to see by faith, and embrace the Saviour that *was to come;* and in the Gospel Church, till a man be baptized " with the Holy Ghost and with fire," the eyes of his mind, though he be a partaker of water Baptism, are equally closed to the glories, and careless of the salvation, of the Saviour that *has come.*

From these views of the subject we conclude that the analogical argument from circumcision to Baptism, when logically followed out, condemns instead of affords support to the views of our Oxford brethren.

We need not say that they can derive no support from the incidental texts which we have already quoted, from which it is inferred, but from which it cannot be positively known, that Baptism was administered to infants by immediate Apostolical direction. Indeed, the fact of circumcision being so positively enjoined upon infants born in the Jewish Church, and yet not conveying that Regeneration of heart, which was as necessary for salvation in that Church as under the Gospel dispensation, while the Baptism of infants is not once enjoined in the New Testament Scriptures, affords very strong presumptive evidence that no such momentous distinction between the two ordinances exists as that for which our opponents contend. It is hardly possible to conceive, that if it were intended to communicate to the Christian Church a privilege of such surpassing and infinite value—a privilege hitherto unheard of and unimagined, namely, that she should, in the act of Baptism, impart the hidden life of God to every *infant*,—no intimation of the invaluable gift and unexampled grace should be distinctly offered in the Word of God.

The third ground on which, taken in connexion with the others, we have stated that the practice of infant Baptism may be satisfactorily defended, is the history of the primitive Christian Church.

And here it is important to advert to a very obvious, but too frequently forgotten distinction, in considering the value of the writings of the early Fathers. In respect to a fact such as this, it is their testimony as to its existence and its prevalence, not the opinions they entertained respecting it, that makes their authority of any weight or validity. We have the *practice*, and we have the *fact*, that amidst innumerable differences of opinion on other subjects, they never doubted or disputed about this, which appears well nigh impossible, had it not been countenanced and practised by the Apostolic Churches. But their opinions in respect of doctrines constitutes obviously a distinct matter, and rests on a distinct foundation, and is to be tried by a different test. Certain appropriate and well-understood evidence proves an historical fact. An alleged Christian doctrine can be established, not by evidence of this kind, but by its coincidence with the one invariable and perfect standard. The practice and history of the early Church forms a complete evidence of the *fact* of infant Baptism being practised from the earliest times. Their judgment as to the truth which *the practice* teaches, remains to be compared with, and tested by Scripture.

The attempt of Professor Pusey to give the character of "divine authority" to *the views* of the early Fathers on this and other matters, is one of the most improper, and, we ought to add, extravagant propositions which these Tracts contain. Not only do we find in the Apostolic times a whole Church deceived by the extraordinary extravagance, that unless Gentile converts should be circumcised and should keep the law of Moses they could not be saved; but what is still more to our purpose, we hear the great Apostle declaring, that "the mystery of iniquity" which was to produce the "Man of Sin," "the Son of Perdition," did in his time "already work;" and he forewarns the bishops of the Church of Ephesus, that after his departure, "of *their* ownselves should men arise, speaking perverse things, to draw away disciples after them;" while the beloved Apostle records, before *his* departure, at a later period, that there were, even then, in the Church "*many Antichrists.*" History records the different strange and unfounded doctrines, which were soon introduced into, and received by the Church, after the departure of the Apostles. To this branch of the subject we shall presently recur. In the meantime we shall simply refer to one practice of the primitive Church, which of itself shows how little it is entitled to the divine honour with which Professor Pusey is disposed to invest it.

Wheatly on the Common Prayer says (at chap. ix. page 394), "In the *primitive Church*, indeed, such persons as were baptised in the presence of the bishop, were immediately presented to him in order for *confirmation.* Nor was this only true with respect to adult persons, but also with regard to infants, who, if a bishop was present, were frequently *confirmed* immediately upon their baptism; (!) as may be shown from direct testimony of the ancients, as well as *that known usage or custom*, of giving the *Holy Eucharist to infants* (*! !*) which ordinarily supposes their confirmation." * The same is practised by the Greek Church to this day. †

We conclude, then, that this reference to the word of God on the subject of *infant* Baptism, whether it be made directly to the text of Scripture, or more indirectly by analogy to circumcision, instead of weakening the conclusion which we had previously reached by contrasting the character of Professor Pusey's regenerate ones with that of the truly regenerate, as depicted by the pen of inspiration, only strengthens and confirms it, and proves by another process that Baptismal Regeneration is not the doctrine of Scripture; while the slight reference which we have made to the early Fathers is confirmatory of the opinion which we have already expressed, and promise presently satisfactorily to establish, that their decision on many disputed theological questions (and this of the number) is not entitled to be quoted with peculiar respect.

We are thus brought, in relation to the subject of Infant Baptism, to the consideration of the last authority of immediate interest to our readers, namely, that of our own Church.

In the last chapter we considered the views of the Church on the subject, as given in the Twenty-fifth and Twenty-seventh Articles (on *the Sacraments* and *on Baptism*). We consider that these Articles refer to the Sacraments exclusively as administered to *adults :* that as

---

* See both these points proved in Mr. Bingham's " Antiquities of the Christian Church," vol. iv. p. 368.

† See Dr. Smith's " Account of the Greek Church," p. 116.

our Church does not follow the superstitious, and we must add, the *profane* practice of the early Church in administering *the Lord's Supper* to infants, and consequently the observations more immediately referring to that Sacrament could not apply to *them*, so as it regards the Sacrament of Baptism, the last clause of the Twenty-seventh Article appears to limit the application of the previous clauses of the Article to adults. Our readers know well the terms of that clause. After the Article has stated what Baptism is not and what it is (in the words whose import we formerly considered), it closes as follows:—" The Baptism of young children is in any wise to be retained in the Church *as most agreeable* with the institution of Christ."

That this is the correct view of the subject is, we think, also shown by the clause in the Article immediately preceding that just quoted, in which the benefits last narrated as received by the faithful recipient of Baptism are stated in these words:—" *Faith is confirmed and grace increased* by virtue of prayer unto God." This clause obviously is framed on the supposition, 1st, that faith previously existed in the recipient, for that cannot be " confirmed" which does not previously exist, and also that he was, previous to Baptism, a recipient of grace, for neither can that be " *increased*" which has no existence. This clause accordingly proves, what the last clause of the Article indicates, that the definition of Baptism contained in the whole Article is not intended to apply to *infant* Baptism; while it cuts up, root and branch, the theory of our Oxford brethren on the subject, inasmuch as it authoritatively states, not that Baptism is the instrument of *conferring* or *infusing the grace* of God, but only of *increasing* it.

Upon the whole, this declaratory announcement of our Church, in her " ARTICLES OF RELIGION," which " contain the true doctrine of the Church of England, agreeable to God's word," is at once scriptural, guarded, significant, and instructive. Infant Baptism is to be retained in the Church, not, let it be observed, in consequence of the command of Christ, or as the institution of Christ, or as the appointed and infallible instrument of making infants " the sons of God," but " as *most agreeable* with the institution of Christ."

So far, then, as to the bearing of THE ARTICLES on the subject of infant Baptism.

In relation to the two services of the Church which more immediately bear upon infant Baptism, and which tend to confuse the minds of many men on the subject, and to withdraw them from the simplicity of the Gospel—namely, the Baptismal Service and the Catechism—even these services if carefully examined, are very far from supporting the views of our Oxford brethren.

They hold, we have seen, that the virtue of Baptism in regenerating the soul cannot be *affected* by the faith, or desires, or prayers of any one, but that in the ordinance, the Church absolutely infuses, without any dependence on these, the divine life into every infant. But this is not assumed in these services. The very reverse is, in fact, taken for granted and asserted. So completely is this the case, that the ordinance would not be administered at all, except under the profession by the sureties of the child, in his name, of faith and a renunciation of the devil, the world, and the flesh; and if that promise is made ignorantly or lightly, or not confirmed by the child when he comes to the years of discretion, the inevitable consequence is, that the whole falls to the ground. In support of this view, let us observe that the Church directs, in the 29th Canon, that none but those who are in full communion with the Church shall be admitted to act as Godfathers or Godmothers to an infant; and her statement is absolute that the child is " verily bound to believe and to do as they have promised" in his name. If an adult were lightly, and without faith, to profess to believe, and promise to obey the Gospel, would the Sacrament administered to him by the Church, *in consequence of his profession and promise*, be of any value to him? Assuredly not. And if the confession and promise of the sureties be made in the name of the child lightly and without faith, and their confession and promise, so made, be never fulfilled by the child when he reaches the years of discretion, whence does the Church in the one case derive a power to convey a gift of surpassing value which she cannot impart in the other? And this question may be put with the stronger emphasis, when it is considered that even a simple and direct authority to impart the outward ordinance to children is not conveyed to her in the word of God. The Church, assuredly, assumes for herself no such power; we are convinced she is invested with none such in Scripture.

Did this view of the subject require confirmation, it would receive it abundantly by a reference to two other services of our Church, namely, that of Confirmation and of the Burial of the Dead.

In the former of these, *after those about to be confirmed have taken their Baptismal vows on themselves*, the Bishop commences prayer as follows:—" Almighty and everlasting God, *who hast vouchsafed to regenerate these thy servants by water and the Holy Ghost, and hast given unto them forgiveness of all their sins*." Here, obviously, there is as absolute a declaration of regeneration by the Spirit and forgiveness of sins as in the service for infant Baptism. But it will be confessed by all, that these words used by the Church, are only the words of charity, resting on the foundation of the confession by the individual now come to the years of discretion, of a lively faith in Christ, and of his having " renounced the devil and all his works, the vain pomps and glory of the world, with all the covetous desires of the same, and the carnal desires of the flesh," being just and true. Without such confession, no minister of a Christian Church, whose conscience was not seared as with a hot iron, would venture to declare, in the case of an adult, the remission of sins, or to pronounce that the heart was regenerated by the operation of the Holy Ghost. But if the confession is false—if there be no true faith in Christ, and no real renunciation of the world—the individual, by universal confession, instead of being pardoned or accepted of God, is only involving himself in deeper guilt by the solemn mockery. No Protestant divine, nor Popish either we presume, will hesitate to admit the accuracy of this statement. Here, then, is there in words the most absolute and unrestricted assertion on the part of the Church of regeneration and pardon, but resting, confessedly, on the TRUTH of that profession, without which they would never have been uttered.

And so, as it regards the Burial Service. In that sublime composition the following statement is made:—" Forasmuch as it hath pleased God of *his great mercy to take unto himself the soul* of our dear brother here departed." On what foundation does this absolute statement rest, that God has, of *his great mercy, taken to himself* the soul of the departed, but on the like supposition as that to which we have referred in the Confirmation Service, namely, that his profession of Christianity was a true and genuine one? If it were not so, then no service can alter the fact that he has been taken away, not in mercy, but in wrath; and instead of his soul being taken to God, it has been for ever separated from him. We presume there is no Protestant, deserving of the name, who will deny this solemn truth.

If, then, in these two services the most absolute statements are made, resting, however, in both on a supposition beyond human observation, on what principle of reason or common sense are we called upon to believe that in the use of similar absolute language in the service appointed for the Baptism of Infants, the Church expresses herself to another effect: especially, when this absolute language is used only AFTER a similar promise is made in the name of the infant, and accompanied by the statement that the child is " verily bound to believe, and to do as they have promised?"

We are aware that our High Church brethren have adopted the following dogma on the subject,—that where, as in the case of an unconscious infant, no mental opposition is offered to the administration of the ordinance, in this case it ever proves efficacious for the new creation of God in the soul. But when we ask for Scriptural authority for this assertion, we ever ask in vain. It is a mere baseless assertion. We assert, that as it is unsupported by the letter of Scripture, it is equally opposed to its whole spirit, and that the more it is viewed in the light of the word of God, the more will it be seen to be a most false, and a most hurtful theory.

To conclude this branch of the subject—the services themselves, *in so far as many of their statements are made to rest on a bare supposition or contingency,* we do not admire. And inasmuch as we are persuaded they have led many into error, and that much misconception and mystification, especially on the subject of Baptismal Regeneration, have had their origin in their peculiar construction, we think their reduction into a simpler form is much to be desired. But an improvement of this kind is more to be desired than expected; and we must submit to receive a lesson even from the formularies of our Church, as from every other thing in the world, that perfection is not a property of any human work. It is only when that which is perfect is come, that that which is in part shall be done away. This, however, is certain, that the terms of these services, justly considered, do anything rather than countenance the erroneous opinions of Professor Pusey and his Oxford friends, and this undoubtedly is a cause of pleasure and thanksgiving.

CHAPTER V.

THE SACRAMENT OF THE LORD'S SUPPER.

THE union of Christ with his people is of the most intimate description; and, for wise purposes, the strongest language, and images the most striking and comprehensive, are employed in Scripture to impress our minds with its entireness and perfection. It is not only exhibited to us as that of the Vine and the branches, as that of the Head with the members of the Body, but as that of the Father with the Son:—"that they may be all one," says the Divine Saviour, "as thou, Father, art in me, and I in thee, that they also may be one in us." Speaking "concerning Christ and the Church," the Apostle says, " For we are members of his body, of his flesh, and of his bones."

This is not our state by nature. Since the fall of our first parents, we are " by nature *the children of wrath.*" This state is obviously as far as possible removed from that of *the children of God,* whose condition is pourtrayed by the images to which we have just referred ; and it is difficult or impossible for the imagination to conceive a change more vast than that which takes place in man upon his regeneration by the Spirit of God.

One of the fundamental errors, as it regards this class of subjects, entertained by the writers whose opinions we combat, and an error from which much confusion and distress is occasioned to many incomparably better instructed in the truth than they, is that which applies the above sublime truths to the union of Christ with his outward and visible Church. No conception can be more false, and few more offensive (from the complete incongruity, between the image and the reality) to every truly enlightened mind. The term *Church* has different significations. In its highest signification, it points at that glorious company which constitute Christ's mystical body. It is this company of which it is said, " And gave him to be head over all things to the *Church,* which is his body" (Eph. i. 22) ; and again, " That he might present to himself a glorious *Church,* not having spot, or wrinkle, or any such thing" (Eph. v. 27), and which is pointed out in various other passages of Scripture of similar import.

It is to the Church, so defined, that the promises of God, as to its safety and durability, are addressed. Not to any outward division or section of it, but to the living members, individually and collectively, of Christ's mystical body, whose " life is hid with Christ in God." It is against THIS BODY, composed of innumerable living members, against which the gates of hell shall never prevail. To any particular body of Christians the promise does not apply. Where are now the seven Churches of Asia? where are the African Churches? Perished. Where is the once-flourishing Church of Rome ? It is in a state incomparably worse than if it had outwardly perished. It is apostate. " The gates of hell" have prevailed against the others to destroy them: against this they have prevailed to render it the minister and instrument of Satan. But THE CHURCH lives; and whatever changes may still occur in the outward state and circumstances of the different Christian communities of which it is composed, it must endure till the spiritual temple, as it stands complete in the Divine Mind and purpose, shall be perfected, and the head stone be at last brought forth with shoutings.

This spiritual temple, so constituted, so honoured, and so secured by promises which cannot fail, is reared after the manner of buildings in this world. Each separate stone is brought out of the quarry of this world, and formed for its proper place by the Divine Architect. And no other power than His who can give life to the dead, and call things that are not into being, is equal to the production of these living stones. No, although in the Romish Apostacy, or in our own Church, or any Church that exists, or ever has existed, or ever shall exist, the individual may have been a participator of both Sacraments —may have been baptized, as well as eaten and drunk in Christ's name, yet if not born of the Spirit—if not baptized by " the Holy Ghost as with fire "— the decision of the Saviour is clear and impressive—" I NEVER *knew you :*" a statement utterly irreconcileable with the supposition that at one time, by the administration of the Sacrament of Baptism, he was in very deed a member of Christ's mystical body.

In the general, a change so momentous, so fundamental, so comprehensive as that of being "delivered from the power of darkness, and translated into the kingdom of God's dear Son " (Col. i. 13), is well known to the subject of it ; and when he is made sensible of it, he is called upon to give "thanks to God the Father" on this account. "If any man be in Christ, he is a *new* creature : old things are passed away ; behold, all things are become *new*." (2 Cor. v. 17.) "For ye were sometimes *darkness,* but now are ye *light* in the Lord." (Ephes. v. 8.) "That ye should shew forth the praises of Him who hath called you out of *darkness* into his marvellous *light*." (1 Peter ii. 9.) Such texts are used in Scripture equally as it respects Jewish and Gentile converts, and they are equally appropriate when applied to the regeneration or conversion of nominal Christians. Take a respectable Hindu, a respectable Jew, and a respectable baptized nominal Christian, and it is wonderful how little essential difference of character is to be found among them. Less, we venture to say, than the very different systems of education which they have severally received would lead us to anticipate ; while the existence of any such momentous distinction and opposition of character as that pronounced in the Word of God, in the texts just given, as severing regenerate from unregenerate men, it were a manifold folly and absurdity to assert. No ! men awfully misinterpret and pervert Scripture — they awfully deceive themselves and wofully deceive others, when they allege that all Christians are in Baptism made partakers of the New Birth of the Gospel. There are those, no doubt, who, under the Gospel as under the Jewish dispensation, are sanctified from their mothers' womb, and those who in Baptism or in childhood are made partakers of the Divine nature; so that in after life they see their New Birth most strikingly by the contrast of their character with that of worldly men, and by its agreement with the descriptions of the new creature given in the word of God. But these form the exceptions and not the rule, and according to the usual dispensations of the Spirit, the change, whether more quickly or more gradually effected, is such that the regenerate person can eventually adopt the language of the man delivered from his natural blindness by our Lord, and say, " One thing I know, that whereas I was blind, now I see."

The agent in effecting the New Birth in man is acknowledged by all to be the Spirit of God, and he works by producing in the subjects of his gracious operations, faith, and repentance, that is, a change of will, affections, object, and purpose. Instead of being whole, the subject of Divine grace now finds himself spiritually sick—instead of being strong in his own righteousness, or resolutions, or purposes, he finds himself utterly weak and helpless—he perceives that Christ is the only and the all-sufficient Saviour of sinners such as he feels himself to be—he is assured that if he come to him, he will in no wise cast him out—he does come to him—he does rest upon him—in him he finds rest to his soul, and eventually perceives that he "is made of God unto *him*, wisdom, and righteousness, and sanctification, and redemption "—that he is complete in Christ—that without him he can do nothing—that he can do all things through Christ which strengtheneth him. All these *new* things are perceived by FAITH alone—by that faith whose operations and effects are so strikingly pourtrayed in the eleventh chapter of the Hebrews—even that faith which overcometh the world. " This is the victory that *overcometh the world,* even *our faith.*" " Whatsoever is born of God *overcometh the world.*" Wherefore, whoever hath faith is born of God.

The Christian being regenerated and born of God, proceeds steadily in his endeavours to walk " in all the commandments and ordinances of the Lord blameless." Supposing him an adult, not having received Baptism in infancy, and now believing in Christ " *with all his heart,*" which is an indispensable pre-requisite to the administration of the ordinance (Acts viii. 37, 38), he comes and is baptized according to Christ's command and appointment, and he finds the ordinance a means of grace — an instrument, rightly improved, of stablishing, strengthening, settling him. Or if he has been baptized in infancy, he will find in the solemn consideration of the promises and vows, in virtue of which he was made a participator of the Sacrament, much to strengthen and settle his resolutions to be entirely devoted in soul, body, and spirit to Him who in mercy has revealed himself to his soul.

But besides the Sacrament of Baptism, there is that of the Lord's Supper, and to the consideration of that holy ordinance we must now devote a little consideration.

This Sacrament is unquestionably a great and important means of grace, but, in our judgment, there is a strong tendency, among High Churchmen, to view it superstitiously : to treat it in essence, though not in form, after the manner of Rome. A serious error in our Church in the present day, is stated in the advertisement to the second volume of the *Tracts for the Times*, to be, "the *a priori* reluctance in those who believe the Apostolic commission *to appropriate to it the power of consecrating* the Lord's Supper; as if there were some antecedent improbability in God's gifts being lodged in particular observances, and *distributed in a particular way ;* and as if the strong wish, or moral worth, of the individual could create in the outward ceremony a virtue which it had not received from above." And again, " Indeed this may be set down as the essence of sectarian doctrine to consider faith, and not *the Sacraments as the instrument of Justification and other Gospel gifts :* instead of holding, that the grace of Christ comes to us altogether from without (who holds otherwise ?), (as from Him, so through externals of his ordaining,) faith being but the *sine quâ non*, the *necessary condition on our parts* for duly receiving it."

The institution of the Lord's Supper is narrated by the three first Evangelists in terms so simple, that it is difficult to suppose how, from these narratives at least, the superstitious notions should have originated which had their perfection in transubstantiation, but which were exhibited also in consubstantiation, and in many other of the fancies which have been excogitated on the subject in various ages, and which seem now to have obtained a resting-place in the minds of our Oxford brethren.

To take the narrative of St. Luke, he says, "And he took bread, and gave thanks, and brake it, and gave unto them, saying, This is my body which is given for you : this do *in remembrance of me.* Likewise also the cup after supper, saying, This cup is the new testament in my blood, which is shed for you." The body of our blessed Lord was still unbroken, not a drop of his precious blood had been shed, but in the bread and wine was there a representation of his body that was to be broken, and his blood that was to be shed for us, and " this do," says he, " *in remembrance of me.*" A most affecting and most loving injunction, but the conception that it was to be " *the instrument of justification*" is certainly as far as possible from being contained in the words.

The well-known passage in the eleventh chapter of 1 Corinthians is a very important one, as exhibiting the true nature of the ordinance, and in divesting it of the superstitious character with which our High Church brethren would invest it.

The Corinthians, it appears, had dreadfully abused the Sacrament. They came together as to a common meal; and, it would seem, the principles of charity, and even of *temperance*, were forgotten by them when professing to eat the Lord's Supper—" One *was hungry*, and another *was drunken*," while in their revelry they neglected and shamed their poor and destitute brethren. In such circumstances, we may be assured the Apostle would give as distinct and impressive an insight into the true nature and objects of the ordinance, and in what its essence consisted, as could be done; and this he does in the following words:—

" For I have received of the Lord that which also I delivered unto you, That the Lord Jesus the same night in which he was betrayed took bread: and when he had given thanks, he brake it, and said, Take, eat: this is my body, which is broken for you: *this do in remembrance of me.* After the same manner also he took the cup, when he had supped, saying, This cup is the new testament in my blood: this do ye, as often as ye drink it, *in remembrance of me.* For as often as ye eat this bread, and drink this cup, *ye do shew the Lord's death till he come.* Wherefore whosoever shall eat this bread, and drink this cup of the Lord, unworthily, shall be guilty of the body and blood of the Lord. But let a man examine himself, and so let him eat of that bread and drink of that cup. For he that eateth and drinketh unworthily, eateth and drinketh damnation to himself, not discerning the Lord's body."

In this interesting passage the object of the Sacrament is stated three times—twice in the words of our Lord, and once in those of the Apostle. Our Lord first, in giving the bread, says, " this do *in remembrance of me;* " and again, after delivering the cup, " this do ye, as oft as ye drink it, *in remembrance of me;* " and the Apostle, in conformity with the declaration of Christ, says, uniting the two parts of the Sacrament into one, " For as often as ye eat this bread and drink this cup, *ye do shew forth the Lord's death till he come.* " How passing strange—how utterly incomprehensible, if the High Church dictum were correct, that "*the Sacraments are the instruments of justification and other Gospel gifts*," that our Lord, in the original institution of the ordinance, and the Apostle, in explaining to the erring Corinthians the nature of the thing they had profaned, should give no hint of its incomparably most important purpose and object!—Having stated the primary and leading object of the Sacrament in the words of our Lord, and in his own as inspired by the Spirit, the Apostle proceeds to declare the consequences which would follow from so great a profanation as had been common among the Corinthians. As it regarded those who partook of the ordinance, carelessly and profanely, or without faith to discern the Lord's body, they would be guilty of the body and blood of the Lord; their guilt would be of the same character as that of those who " trampled under foot the Son of God, and counted the blood of the covenant with which he (Christ) was sanctified an unholy thing, and did despite to the Spirit of grace ;" and thus, instead of deriving profit from the sacred feast, they would eat and drink condemnation to themselves.

Notwithstanding this plain and most distinct explanation of the object of the Lord's Supper, given not by early Fathers and fallible men, but by our Lord himself and his inspired Apostle, multitudes have ever had a strong tendency to look with a superstitious eye on this Sacrament, and to conceive that in partaking of the body and blood of Christ there was some hidden virtue communicated, *altogether distinct from that which Christ by his Spirit imparts to his people in the other ordinances of his grace.* But this is surely a mistake; and the fact that in the account of the institution of the ordinance given by the Evangelists, and repeated with more particularity by St. Paul, the primary object of the institution should *alone* be mentioned, to the *exclusion* of those other effects which we find realised by it, (in that it has proved a most important means of grace and source of consolation and strength to the true Church in all ages,) seems to have been so ordered as a preventative of that evil into which men are so prone to fall, and into which they have so recklessly and lamentably sunk in respect of this ordinance, notwithstanding this merciful check and palpable hindrance.

But let us now consider the language which our Church uses in regard to this Sacrament.

The doctrine of Scripture on the subject appears to be stated with great propriety and truth in the Twenty-eighth Article, in the following words :—

" The Supper of the Lord is not only a sign of the love that Christians ought to have among themselves one to another; but rather is a Sacrament of our redemption by Christ's death: insomuch that to such as rightly, worthily, and with faith receive the same, the bread which we break is a partaking of the body of Christ; and likewise the cup of blessing is a partaking of the blood of Christ."

" The body of Christ is given, taken, and eaten, in the Supper, only after an heavenly and spiritual manner. And the mean whereby the body of Christ is received and eaten in the Supper is Faith."

We find in these words that to true communicants " the bread which we break is a partaking of the body of Christ; and likewise the cup of blessing is a partaking of the blood of Christ:" moreover, that this partaking of the body and blood of Christ is " only after an heavenly and spiritual manner," and that the means whereby it is truly partaken of " is FAITH." And if we recur to the images to which we pointedly referred at the beginning of this chapter, employed by the Spirit to convey to our minds the complete and perfect union which subsists between Christ and the members of his mystical body —the image of the vine and the branches, of the head and members of the body—if we refer to that astonishing statement made by the Apostle when not treating at all of the Eucharist, " for we are members of his body, of his flesh, and of his bones"—we shall perceive how the whole spiritual and regenerated Church stands complete in Christ as one body, constituting " the fulness of him who filleth all in all" (Eph. i. 23), and in what harmony with other Scriptures, we may be justly said in the Supper, " after an heavenly and spiritual manner," to eat and drink the body and the blood of him who is the only sustenance of our souls, and " the Head of all things to his Church, which is his body."

The true Christian " being justified by faith," and having thus obtained " peace with God through our Lord Jesus Christ;" having obtained " access *by faith* into this grace wherein we stand" (Rom. v. 1. 2), hears his Saviour's voice addressing him, " *Do this in remembrance of me.*" Without that faith, which overcometh the world and constitutes him a child of God, it were impossible he could approach with acceptance the sacred board; for " without faith it is impossible to please Him;" without faith it were impossible " to discern the Lord's body;" and it is only as a living member of the mystical body of Christ that, in the nature of things, he can draw spiritual sustenance from his Divine Head.

He obeys this command given in circumstances so moving. He is already by faith united to Christ. He is " a member of his body, of his flesh, and of his bones;" and over the memorials of the broken body and shed blood of his Lord, he receives spiritual, but most real, sensible, and life-giving communications from his Divine Head;—he becomes a partaker of his body and blood;—he receives new impartations of the only sustenance of his spiritual nature;—and in the use of this, and of the other means of grace of his Saviour Christ's appointment, " he grows up into him in all things, which is his head, even Christ; from whom the whole body fitly joined together and compacted by that which every joint supplieth, groweth into a holy temple in the Lord."

This is our judgment of the Sacrament of the Lord's Supper—of its position and purposes in the economy of grace—and of the manner in which it is to be received, to the nourishment of Christ's mystical body.

Our Oxford brethren, however, consider they have discovered a method by which they effectually neutralise and dissipate all such views as these. They seem to consider they have primitive antiquity on which to rest, and indeed refer, as a proof that their opinion possesses this venerable basis, to the practice of the early Church of administering this Sacrament to infants, and to persons in the article of death, though wholly insensible. But whether it be an ancient conception or a modern invention, we pronounce it a most unscriptural and dangerous error, and one which ought to be loathed and abhorred by every Christian.

The ground on which this error rests is, that faith does not justify us, but the Sacraments; that it is *not* " with *the heart* that man *believeth* unto righteousness, and with the mouth confession is made unto salvation," but that the Sacraments are " THE INSTRUMENTS OF JUSTIFICATION," and that faith is only " the *sine quâ non*, the necessary condition on our parts for duly receiving it" (justification). But we shall give a passage to bring the views of our Oxford brethren on this point distinctly before our readers, although we have already partially extracted it both in this, and in a previous chapter.

At the close of the well-considered advertisement affixed to the second volume of the Tracts, dated OXFORD, the Feast of All Saints, 1835, is the following passage :—

" Hence we have almost embraced the doctrine, that God conveys grace only through the instrumentality of the mental energies, that is, through faith, prayer, active spiritual contemplations, or (what is called) communion with God, in contradiction to the primitive view, according to which the Church and her Sacraments are the ordained and direct visible means of conveying to the soul what is in itself supernatural and unseen. For example, would not most men maintain, on the first view of the subject, that to administer the Lord's Supper to infants, or to the dying and insensible, however consistently pious and believing in their past lives, was a superstition? and yet both practices have the sanction of primitive usage. And does not this account for the prevailing indisposition to admit that Baptism conveys regeneration? Indeed, this may even be set down as the essence of Sectarian doctrine (however its mischief may be restrained or compensated, in the case of individuals), to consider faith, and not the Sacraments, as the *instrument of justification* and other Gospel gifts; instead of holding, that the grace of Christ comes to us altogether from without (as from Him, so through externals of his ordaining), faith being but the *sine quâ non*, the necessary condition on our parts for duly receiving it."

On this most extraordinary passage we observe—

That faith is not only " the *necessary condition* on our part for receiving justification," but it is the means by which we are justified, it is the hand by which we lay hold of Christ to justification," or, as Luther says, " Faith alone, before works, and without works, *appropriates* the benefits of redemption, which is no other than our justification or deliverance from (the condemnation of) sin." Faith unites us to Christ. Every thing is ready on the part of God for the reception of the sinner, through the salvation accomplished for him by Christ. But man either will not believe it, or is wholly indifferent in regard to it. He is careless, asleep, dead, with reference to God and the things which belong to his peace. The Spirit of God quickens those dry bones, (Professor Pusey from this observation must perceive that we hold equally with himself, " that the grace of Christ comes to us altogether from without "), and, becoming a partaker of spiritual life, Christ and his salvation are seen, the need of them is felt, the heart, by faith, rests upon and embraces the Saviour, and his promises of life and salvation, which cannot fail, are *believed*,—and hence, immediately, through the intervention of nothing else, through the simple faith of the soul in the work and promises of the Saviour, the man is justified: " being *justified* by *faith* we have peace with God." The texts in proof of this primary doctrine of the Gospel are innumerable. Let us listen to the words of our Lord himself:—" Jesus saith unto her, I am the resurrection and the life : he that *believeth in me, though he were dead, yet shall he live : and whosoever liveth and believeth in me shall never die.*" May we not solemnly put to every one of our Oxford brethren the question of our Lord which immediately follows—" Believest thou this?"

" *Faith is but a condition. They are the Sacraments which are the instruments of justification,*" says Professor Pusey. Let us try. The Spirit saith, in three distinct passages, (Rom. i. 17, Gal. iii. 11, Heb. x. 38), " The just shall live by FAITH :" Professor Pusey says, " by the Sacraments." The Spirit saith, " purifying their hearts by *faith*" (Acts xv. 9); Professor Pusey says, by the Sacraments. The Spirit saith, "Who are sanctified *by faith* that is in me" (Acts xxvi. 18); Professor Pusey saith, " by the Sacraments ordained by me." The Spirit saith, in various passages, " A man is justified by faith " (Rom. iii. 28, v. 1 ; Gal. ii. 16, iii. 24); Professor Pusey says, Faith is only a condition, and cannot justify—" a man is jus- tified by the Sacraments." The learned Professor says, Faith does not act *instrumentally* at all; the Spirit saith, " Thou *standest* by faith" (Rom. xi. 20), "*walkest* by faith" (2 Cor. v. 7), " *livest* by faith" (Gal. ii. 20), it "removes mountains" (Matt. xvii. 20), it "over- cometh the world " (1 John v. 4), it " *subdues kingdoms, works righteousness, obtains promises, stops the mouths of lions, quenches the violence of fire,*" and so on, recounting mighty deeds of renown, all accomplished through faith as an instrument and source of action. But Professor Pusey says, it cannot be; " Faith is only a *condition*, and *instrumentally* can do nothing." The Church indeed says (eleventh Article), " that we are JUSTIFIED by *faith only*, is a most wholesome doctrine, and very full of comfort." " But "—the language of our Oxford brethren is, in effect, as follows—" but, the Church has a good deal of the leaven of modern and reforming times," and in this is mistaken. This is, in fact, " the essence of sectarian doctrine," which in this matter the Church has adopted. We are *justified by the Sacraments:* it is this which is the " wholesome doctrine and very full of comfort," and it is to be lamented that the Church has departed from the " primitive usage " of administering the Lord's Supper to infants and the insensible, as " the ordained and direct visible means of conveying to their souls what is in itself supernatural and unseen, as by the retaining of this practice the principle would have been preserved more distinct." To most men, indeed, *on the first view of the subject*, this " primitive usage " might appear "a superstition:" for the direction of our Lord is, " Do this *in remembrance* of me," and the Apostle teaches us we must " have faith to discern the Lord's body ;" but it ought to be considered, as St. Bernard saith, " Great is the faith of the Church (*Tracts*, vol. ii. p. 154), and no doubt, as she can impart faith to infants, so she can impart it to the insensible or the insane."—We wish not to indulge in ridicule with reference to a subject so sacred and so solemn, but our readers will perceive that we do nothing more than expose in a clear light the opinions on this subject of our Oxford brethren.

From all such errors may God in mercy deliver his Church. Man though a fallen, is still, praised be His name, a rational and intel- ligent creature. As such he is addressed by God, reasoned with, reproved, threatened, exhorted, besought, commanded. Had God revealed that it was by the Sacraments we were to be justified, and through these alone to apprehend his salvation, and subsequently to be made partakers of the Saviour, his people would have received the truth, in the exercise of the reason which he has given them, rectified by the operation of his Spirit promised to them who ask him. But he has taught them no such doctrine. He has shown them a more excellent way. And in obedience to the Apostolical in-junction to " prove all things," we try and find that the views of our Oxford brethren are unscriptural and false.

God has accomplished in Jesus Christ, all that is necessary for the restoration and salvation of man. His address to every human being whom the glad tidings of great joy reaches is " ONLY believe;" " *Believe* in the Lord Jesus Christ, and *thou shalt be saved;*" " Come now, and let us reason together, saith the Lord, though your sins be as scarlet, they shall be white as snow; though they be red like crimson, they shall be as wool;" " Ho, every one that thirsteth, come ye to the waters, and he that hath no money; come ye, buy, and eat; yea, come, buy wine and milk without money and without price;" " And the Spirit and the bride say, Come. And let him that heareth say, Come, and let him that is athirst come, and whoso-ever will, let him take the water of life freely." The Saviour of mankind stands with open and outstretched arms, inviting all, without exception, to come unto him and live; to come unto him, that they may have life, and have it abundantly. " Whosoever cometh unto me," saith the compassionate and the Almighty Saviour, " I will *in no wise* cast out."

All that under the Gospel is interposed between God and the sinner is expressed in these words—" Ye *will not* come unto me that ye may have life." Let the will be renewed and the work is done. In this renewal of the will the Spirit employs various instruments, as it pleases him. Sometimes he acts through the word preached or read, sometimes through the advice of friends, or through the afflictive dispensations of God's providence, or by various other instruments, as it pleases Him who worketh in us both " to will and to do of his good pleasure." With the hand of faith the sinner lays hold of the Saviour. He is received and cherished by Him in whom he trusts. Though separated from all the ordinary means and ordinances of grace, though in the deserts of Africa, or the wilds of Siberia, though in the most distant island of the sea, though in the deepest dungeon of the Inquisition, though outcast from the abodes and sympathies of men, though wandering in deserts and on mountains, in dens and caves of the earth, destitute, afflicted, tormented, if *by faith* he has apprehended and trusted in the Saviour of sinners, he is blessed—he receives the sustenance he requires from his living Head—he will never be confounded. And in more ordinary and favourable circumstances—in the use and enjoyment of the word, sacraments, and prayer—he is trained up for the heavenly inheritance. Man, indeed, attempts to straiten and confine the grace and gifts of God within limits of his own devising, and which, however they may be countenanced by " primitive usage," are not to be found in the word of God.   Amidst his own bonds the Apostle rejoiced in the great truth that " the word of God is not bound."   But he could have no such rejoicing now.   It *is* bound.   It is bound to the Apostolic Succession.   If it does not come through the holy Apostolic line, a man may hear the Gospel, believe it, rejoice in it, but he is only lying amidst the uncovenanted mercies of God.   His faith is merely a " necessary condition " on his part, but it is not " the instrument of justification and of other Gospel gifts," and therefore cannot save him. He is still unregenerate.   Whatever he may think, he is no child of God.   Unless he receive Baptism and the Lord's Supper, by a priest in " the holy Apostolic line," he cannot know either that he is " born from above," or that he has received " the Lord's body."   He may have so received it, but he has no *right* to any of the promises that assure him of it.   " The word of God," then, " is now bound."   It is grievously bound.   It is forced within a narrow, aye, and a polluted and defiled channel, and only runs through a circumscribed sphere. But we say most solemnly to those men who would thus bind the word of God,—take heed what you do.   Tremble lest ye " make void *the Gospel* through your TRADITIONS."   *There is no such binding of it in the word of God.   It is by* " TRADITIONS " *alone you bind it.*   Take care you are not found fighting against God, and shutting out his mercy from mankind.   We would not join you in your dark attempt for ten thousand worlds.   We would rather proclaim, during our mortal days, over the circuit of the earth—" WHOSOEVER *calleth upon the name of the Lord Jesus* SHALL *be saved.*"

CHAPTER VI.

WHILE it may be said of most things, it is eminently to be asserted of the truth of God, that one part of it cannot be misconceived and perverted, but the error naturally leads to the corruption of the rest, and the usual consequence is the progress of the gangrene over the entire body of the revelation of God, till it be entirely destroyed and lost. When the late Mr. Irving published his first momentous error in regard to the human nature of our Lord, it was not perceived that it naturally led to the overthrow of the fundamental doctrine of Scripture,—justification through the righteousness of Christ. It did so, however, and before his death, that lamented individual taught that we must stand before God in our own holiness, and repudiated what he called, the huxtering doctrine of Imputation. In this point of view, a solitary error in divine truth (if we can suppose such to exist) is to be dreaded like a solitary sin. As surely as the tendency of the latter, if cherished, is to reduce the whole man under the power of iniquity, so certain is the natural effect of error to propagate error, till truth wither and die under its pestilential influence. This truth, if we mistake not, receives its usual illustration in the progress of the important errors held and promulgated by our Oxford brethren which we have already considered. And to one or two of these we now solicit the attention of our readers.

The grand object of the Gospel is to bring sinners home to the Saviour ; and the object is effected, when, *convinced* of their lost and sinful condition, they come to Christ " by faith," " with their whole heart," acting under the assurance of that Gospel truth " that he is able to save them to the uttermost that come unto God by Him." They then find and feel the promises of the eternal God to be their support. *Faith* they perceive to be " the *substance* of things hoped for." It gives to things unseen the substance of things of whose existence they are assured of by their bodily senses. By Faith they " see Him who is invisible," and rest upon his promises, as a child upon the word of promise, visibly proceeding from the lips of his father, whom he venerates and loves. As the union which subsists between the Saviour and the saved, is represented in Scripture to be of the most intimate description of which the imagination can conceive, so is it experienced to be by the enlightened sinner. He hangs immediately upon the Saviour. There is no creature or thing interposed between them. " Christ is made of God, unto him wisdom, and righteousness, and sanctification, and redemption."

At the close of the last chapter we alluded to the manner in which our Oxford brethren *bound* the word of God, which the Apostle in his days rejoiced was " not bound." Thus all the members of the Continental Churches, whose ministers did not receive ordination from Rome, the entire Church of Scotland, and the whole body of Dissenters, are given over to the " uncovenanted mercies of God," because their pastors do not possess the Apostolical Succession, and accordingly their people have not been regenerated by Baptism rightly administered, nor have their teachers " the body of Christ" to give them. Now, is there any binding having a shadow of approximation to this in the word of God? Why! if by the most unlikely means which it is possible to conceive, the sinner got a sight of the Saviour, and heard of his offers of salvation, and *embraced them*, that man will be saved. " Oh!" say the Oxford divines, " we are not content with holding such language as this,—we have the keys— we and the Romish priests are the only people authorised to preach the Gospel; we alone can impart spiritual regeneration, or give Christ's body to the people; and unless you receive the words and the sacraments as dispensed by us, not one of the promises of Scripture, not one of the blessings of the covenant, are yours. You must be given over to the uncovenanted mercies of God." These are nothing more than the substance of the deliberate assertions of Professor Pusey and his friends. We say there is not a single text in Scripture, rightly understood, which affords ground for these truly Popish assumptions, now adopted by the Oxford divines. THEY LITERALLY MAKE " THE WORD OF GOD OF NONE EFFECT:" and this is done, as by the Jewish Pharisees in a former age, " BY THEIR TRADITIONS."

But men who thus close the door of mercy on mankind in one direction, are not likely to open it aright in any other. It might be anticipated, indeed, that to the favoured sheep of their own fold they would open the rich pastures of Gospel grace and blessings, from which they excluded all others. But this anticipation would not rest on a just and comprehensive knowledge of the Gospel. We shall immediately see that the same misconception of the word of God which excludes from its blessings all who follow not with them, also leads them to cut off, in effect, their own children from its free mercies and rich consolations. Error, as we have said, begets and leads on to error.

This is strikingly exhibited in the doctrines they teach on the subject of REPENTANCE.

Let our readers remember, that in Infant Baptism our Oxford brethren consider all the members of our Church to be born from above and made the children of God; next, that what· they consider "falling away" from the faith appears to be the breaking of a command of the Decalogue; and then perceive from the following extracts, which we give from Professor Pusey's tracts, the melancholy condition in which they place the incomparably largest proportion of the members of our Church; and how, in fact and effect, they rob them, as they previously robbed those who are without, of the precious Gospel of the grace of God. Let them mark how in *their* case also, the plainest, the most important, the most consolatory promises of the Gospel are " rendered of none effect through their traditions." And as they see the two errors, in respect of two classes of men so distinct from each other in the esteem of our Oxford brethren, clasp into and fit together, *depriving both of the treasures of the Gospel freely given by Christ to all,* let them see our views of the ruinous error confirmed and established.

Professor Pusey says :—

" The Fathers urge the difficulty of the cure of sin after Baptism, at the same time that they urge men to seek it : they set side by side the possibility and the pains of repentance : they urge against the Novatian heretic, that there is still ' mercy with God, that He may be feared :' they urge this truth against their own fears, and the insinuations of the evil one, who would suggest hard and desponding thoughts of God, in order to keep in his chain those more energetic spirits, who feel the greatness of their fall, and would undergo any pains whereby they might be restored ; but the Ancient Church consulted at the same time for that more relaxed and listless sort, (of whom the greater part of mankind consist,) who would make the incurring of eternal damnation, the breaking of covenant with God, the forfeiture of His Spirit, the profanation of His Temple (ourselves) a light thing and easy to be repaired. Therefore, while they set forth the greatness of God's mercy, they concealed not the greatness of man's sin, in again defiling what God had anew hallowed : they concealed not *that such a fall was worse than Adam's,* since it was a fall from a higher state and in despite of greater aids : that though God's mercy was ever open, yet it required more enduring pains, more abiding self-discipline, more continued sorrow, *again to become capable of that mercy.*"—(*Tracts for the Times,* vol. ii., p. 57.)

The learned Professor says again :—

" And it behoves us much to ascertain, by patient, teachable study of that word with prayer, whether it be right to make the way of repentance so easy to those who, after Baptism, have turned away from God: whether we have any right at once to appropriate to them the gracious words with which our Saviour invited those who had never known Him, and so had never forsaken Him, and with which, through His Church, He still invites His true disciples to the participation of His own most blessed body and blood—' *Come unto Me*, ye that labour and are heavy laden ;' whether, *having no fresh ' Baptism for the remission of sins' ' to offer, no means of renewing them to repentance,'* we have any right to apply to them the words which the Apostles used in inviting men for the first time into the ark of Christ ; whether we are not thereby making broad the narrow way of life, and preaching ' Peace, Peace,' where, *in this way, at least,* ' there is no peace.' "— (*Ibid.*, vol. ii., p. 207.)

At page 59, Professor Pusey observes :—

" The fountain has been indeed opened to wash away sin and uncleanness, but we dare not promise men a second time the same easy access to it, which they once had : that way is open but once : it were to abuse the power of the keys entrusted to us, again to pretend to admit them thus ; *now there remains only the ' Baptism of tears,'* a Baptism obtained, as the same Fathers said, with much fasting, and with many prayers."

Professor Pusey states in the broadest way, that these sentiments were those of the Primitive Church. He gives various extracts confirmatory of his judgment on this matter. The accuracy of that judgment we are not *at present* going to dispute. We only beg our readers, while they peruse the following extracts from the Fathers to this purpose, that they will form their own opinion of the title of such men to be constituted the sure interpreters of Scripture, and the supreme judges in questions of theology.

The following passage is extracted by Professor Pusey from *Tertullian*, in illustration and confirmation of his principles :—

"' God, providing against these his poisons, though the door of *full oblivion* (ignoscentiæ) is closed, and the bolt of Baptism fastened up, alloweth *somewhat* still to be open. He hath placed in the vestibule (of the Church, where penitents used to kneel) a second repentance, which might be open to those who knock.' But how does Tertullian describe those disciplines? ' Full confession (exomologesis) is the discipline of prostrating and humbling the whole man ; enjoining a conversation which may excite pity ; it enacts as to the very dress and sustenance—to lie on sackcloth and ashes: the body defiled, the mind cast down with grief: those things, in which he sinned, changed by a mournful treatment : for food and drink, bread only and water, for the sake of life, not of the belly: for the most part to nourish prayer by fasting: to groan ; to weep ; to moan day and night before the Lord their God; to embrace the knees of the Presbyters and of the friends of God; to enjoin all the brethren to pray for them. All this is contained in 'full confession,' with the view to recommend their repentance; to honour the Lord by trembling at their peril; by pronouncing on the sinner, to discharge the office of the indignation of God; and by temporal affliction,—I say not to baffle, but—*to blot out eternal torment.* When therefore it rolls them on the earth, it the rather raises them: when it defiles, it cleanses them: accusing, it excuses them: condemning, it absolves them. In as far as thou sparest not thyself, in so far will God, be assured, spare thee.' "—*Ibid.*, p. 60.

St. Chrysostom, on 2 Tim. ii. 25, 26, observes :—

" ' Is, then, repentance excluded? Not repentance, God forbid! but a renewal again by Baptism : for he saith not, "impossible that they should be renewed to repentance," and there stops; but adds, "that they should be renewed," i. e., "become new, *by crucifying again ;*" for "to make men new," belongs only to Baptism ; but the office of Repentance is, when they have been made new, and then become old through sins, to free them from this oldness, and make them new; *but it cannot bring them to that former brightness ;* for then (in Baptism) the whole was grace.' "—*Ibid.*, p. 51.

" He subsequently describes the repentance whereby Christ might again be formed in us, a repentance,—far different from the easy notions of many in modern times,—through condemnation of sin, confession, deep and abiding and abased humility, intense prayer, many tears by night and day, much almsgiving, abandonment of all anger, universal forgiveness, bearing all things meekly." — *Ibid.*, p. 53.

" And this," says Professor Pusey, " is not Chrysostom's opinion only, but that of the ancient Church, that one who shall have fallen grievously after Baptism, though he may ' by God's grace arise and amend his life' (Art. 16), cannot be in the same condition, as if he had never so fallen. . . . . ' God hath set forth Christ Jesus to be a propitiation through faith in his blood, to declare his righteousness for the remission of the sins that are past,' the former sins (τῶν προγεγονότων ἁμαρτημάτων) (Rom. iii. 25), ' the sins of the times of ignorance.' (Acts xvii. 30.) His intercession for sins into which *through the infirmity of the flesh,* though Christians, we may yet fall. ' For these,' St. John, who is manifestly speaking of the sins of true believers, saith, ' we have an Advocate with the Father, Jesus Christ the righteous, and he is the propitiation for our sins:' but we have no account in Scripture of any second remission, obliteration, extinction of all sin, such as is bestowed upon us by ' the one Baptism for the remission of sins.' And that such was the view of the ancient Church, appears the more from the very abuse which we find derived from it; that many, namely, delayed continually the Sacrament of Baptism, (much as persons now do the other Sacrament,) because after they should have received it, they should no more have such full remission. And this unholy frame of mind the Fathers endeavoured to correct, not by denying that they therein held truly, but by setting forth the uncertainty of life, ... but they do not deny, nay, they urge as a ground of very careful and wary walking, that the Baptismal purity, if once soiled, cannot be altogether restored : ' for that there is no second regeneration,' (i. e., second Baptism,) ' no re-formation, no restoration to our former state, yea, though we seek this most earnestly, with many groans and tears; whence there with difficulty (as I at least judge) comes over a certain healing process, which leaves a scar. For this healing does come over (and would that we could efface the scars also! since I too need much mercy), yet is it better to stand in need of no second purification, but to abide by the first, which is, I know, common to all, and without toil— . . . . For it is a fearful thing to bring upon ourselves a laborious for an easy cure; and having cast aside God's pitying grace, to indebt ourselves to chastisement, and set reformation against sin. *For how great tears shall we bring before God, that we may equal the fountain of Baptism ?* "—*Ibid.*, p. 54.

"Epiphanius," says Professor Pusey, "even when writing against the error of the Novatians, still insists, '*In truth it is impossible to renew those who have been once renewed and have fallen away.* For neither can Christ be born again, that He may be crucified for us, nor may any one crucify again the Son of God, who is not again to be crucified, nor can any one receive a second Baptism, for there is one Baptism, and one renewal.' "—*Ibid.*, p. 56.

"I think," says Basil, "that those noble combatants of God, who have during their whole life wrestled thoroughly with the invisible enemies, after they have escaped all their persecutions, and are come *to the end of life*, are examined by the Ruler of this world, that if they be found to have wounds from their contests, or any stain or mark of sin, they may be a while detained [in life];* but if they be found unwounded and unstained, as being invincible and free, they have their rest given them by Christ."—*Ibid.*, p. 57.

"The wounds, then," says Theodoret, "received after Baptism *are* curable; but not as before, in that then remission is given *through faith alone* (the learned Professor must deem this rather an awkward expression) but now through many tears, and mournings, and weepings, and fastings, and prayer, and toil proportioned to the greatness of the sin committed. For we have been taught neither to despair of those thus circumstanced, nor yet readily to impart to them the Holy Rites. 'Give not,' He saith, 'that which is holy to dogs, nor cast the pearls before swine.' "—*Ibid.*, p. 65.

"And, therefore, I say unto you," says Hermas, "that, after that great and holy calling (Baptism) if any be tempted by the devil and sin, he has one repentance. But if he sin again, and repent, it will not profit the man who doth such things, for hardly will he live to God."—*Ibid.* p. 67.

" ' Will any one call that repentance,' " says St. Ambrose, " ' where men seek for worldly dignity, drink wine to the full, or use

---

* This insertion seems by no means to be necessarily implied by the context.

the enjoyments of marriage ? The world must be renounced. Sleep itself must be less indulged than nature requires, must be interrupted by groans, must be sequestrated for prayer. We must live so as to die to this life. Man must deny himself, and be wholly changed.' " —*Ibid.*, p. 63.

We had marked many other passages for quotation, but we think our readers will agree with us in considering that these are amply sufficient. We shall therefore close them with the following summing up of the whole matter by the Rev. Professor :—

" There are, then, these limitations in Scripture, or derived from it by the Fathers, to this second birth *after* Baptism. That it is one of suffering, whereas the former birth, by Baptism, was one of joy and ease ; that it is less complete than the former, and is a slower and more toilsome process (the slowness is spoken of by St. Paul, ' my little children, of whom I travail in birth again, *until Christ be formed in you :'*) that it is a *second* Regeneration, (' of whom I travail *again,'*) —not differing from the preceding, as if the Regeneration of Christ's ordinance were a change of state, the Regeneration of repentance a change of nature ; that, outward in the flesh ; this, inward in the spirit : God forbid that we should so speak of Christ's ordinances !— but that it is a sort of restoration of that life, given to those to whom it is given, by virtue of that ordinance ; a restoration *of a certain portion of their Baptismal health.* It is not ' *the* New Birth' simply ; *that* is Baptism ; but it *is a revival, in a measure, of that life ;* to be received gratefully, as a renewal of a portion of that former gift ; to be exulted in, because it *is* life ; but to be received and guarded with trembling, because it is the renewal of what had been forfeited ; not to be boasted of, because it is but the fragment of an inheritance, ' wasted in riotous living.' *Lastly, it is bestowed through the ministry of the Church.* ' Little children, of whom *I* travail again.' "—*Ibid.*, p. 72.

However objectionable such expressions are in the mouths of the early fathers, and they are undoubtedly *extremely* objectionable, they are, at least as it regards the earlier of them, of a very distinct character in their primary application from that which they assume in the hands of the Oxford divines. As indeed appears from the quotation given above from Gregory Nazianzum, they were primarily applied to cases of *open departures* from the faith by those who in mature life had professed themselves Christians, and received in consequence the sacrament of Baptism. But by Professor Pusey they are, according to the principles of his school, necessarily applied to the cases of every member of the Church of England who has walked unworthy of the Gospel. How MANY MILLIONS there are of these now alive we stop not to inquire. But if we look at the practices of boys at our public schools—if we have any knowledge of the state of morals in the courts of law, in the schools of medicine, in the army and navy, in the busy haunts of business, in the gay and fashionable and dissipated circles of society, among the lower orders of society both in the manufacturing and agricultural divisions of the kingdom; if we have means of knowing, moreover, even where morals are outwardly correct, the general neglect of God and of his ordinances by the population at large, so that the number of our people who " show forth the Lord's death till he come," in comparison of the general mass, is awfully few—the multitude, of all ranks, thus showing most significantly that they put Christ "from them, and judge themselves unworthy of everlasting life," we shall perceive at once in what state the Oxford divines place the immensely greater proportion of their countrymen. What, we ask, is that state? Apostasy. According to Professor Pusey, they all became by water-Baptism partakers of " the New Birth"—they became " the sons of God," they were regenerated in a higher and nobler sense than were " Noah, Daniel, and Job." That the great mass of the population have departed from this grace, we presume it is impossible for Professor Pusey and his friends, according to their principles, to deny. They are thus apostates, and all the statements which the above extracts contain, apply, in all their force and intensity, to the great mass of our countrymen.

However they repent, repentance "cannot bring *them* to that former brightness." (See page 67.) They cannot draw consolation from the fact that " if any man sin, we have an advocate with the Father, Jesus Christ the righteous, and he is the propitiation for our sins;" "for we have no account in Scripture of any second remission, obliteration, extinction of all sin, such as is bestowed upon us by the one baptism for the remission of sins." (See page 67.) Their " baptismal purity cannot be altogether restored;" " having cast aside God's pitying grace, they must be adopted to chastisement, and *set reformation against sin*. For how great tears shall they bring before God, *that they may equal the fountain of baptism*." (See page 68.) They must indeed ponder the saying of Epiphanius, and draw such consolation from it as they can, that " *in truth it is impossible to renew those who have been once renewed and have fallen away*." (See page 68.) They must ponder the saying of the Oxford divines themselves, that " their fall is worse than Adam's, since it was a fall from a higher state, and in despite of greater aids—that though God's mercy is ever open, yet it requires more enduring pains, more abiding self-discipline, more continued sorrow, again to *become capable of mercy*." (See page 65.) And again, an " easy access" to the way of life " is open but once: it were to abuse the power of the keys entrusted to us, again to pretend to admit them thus; now, there remains only the ' baptism of tears,' a baptism obtained with much fasting and with many prayers." (See page 66.) But why do we proceed with this repetition? Let our readers consider anew, if necessary, the other extracts given above, from Tertullian, Theodoret, Hermas, Ambrose, and Professor Pusey himself, and consider how far and how deeply the great bulk of the English nation is removed by our Oxford brethren from the offers of pardon and peace contained in the Gospel; and let them judge whether, while they place those who do not enjoy an Apostolical ministry among the uncovenanted mercies of God, they do not reduce those nominally within the pale of the Church to even a more wretched and helpless condition? If they bind the word of God to those that are without, they surely bind it with equal carefulness as it respects the vast majority of those that are within. We bless God that " the power of the keys," which they so recklessly assume, is possessed as little by them as by his Holiness at Rome. " To the law and to the testimony: *if they speak not according to this word, it is because there is no light in them.*"

An apostate from the profession of the Gospel is certainly in a most awful state. The distinction between an apostate and a backslider, it would be apart from our present subject to investigate and point out: but it is one which our Oxford brethren would do well to inquire into and endeavour to comprehend, before they attempt to instruct the Church on this and other collateral subjects. But without being tempted to enter into different fields of inquiry which this subject naturally opens, we would only at present refer to one view of the subject, which, if it does not convince *them* of their deep error in thus attempting to limit and frustrate the grace of the Gospel, will at least serve to put this truth in a clear point of view before the eyes of our readers. We allude to the fact, that if the views of the Oxford divines are correct, the privileges of the Jewish Church were, in this most essential particular, incomparably higher than those of the Christian; for the Jews, after the most heinous departures from God and outrageous breaking of his holy covenant, were assured of the fullest and freest pardon, and the return of THE BRIGHTNESS of God's favour upon them, *if they would only return;* while we see, that under the perfected system of the Gospel, as interpreted by our Oxford brethren, it remains a doubtful matter, however Christians return to God upon sin after baptism, whether they will be accepted at all; and, undoubtedly, they can never be restored to their " baptismal purity." One would suppose, from the use they make of the Gospel, that the saying of our Lord was, " *Grace* came by Moses, but the *Law* by Jesus Christ." How much more blessed the *Law* as enjoyed by the Jews, than the *Gospel* as perverted by Professor Pusey!

Let us listen to God speaking to backsliding Israel and Judah— " Ah, sinful nation," "laden with iniquity," " they have forsaken the Lord, they have provoked the Holy One of Israel to anger." " From the sole of the foot even unto the head, there is no soundness in it, but wounds, and bruises, and putrefying sores." Here is their condition laid open by God himself. In what language, then, does the divine mercy address these wretched outcasts? " Come, now, *let us reason together, saith the Lord ;* though your sins be as *scarlet,* they *shall be as white as snow* (is there any lack of purity, lustre, or brightness here?); though they be red like *crimson,* they shall be as *wool.*"— (Isaiah i.)

Let us listen again—" But thou hast not called upon me, O Jacob; but thou hast been weary of me, O Israel." " *Thou hast made me to serve with thy sins, thou hast wearied me with thine iniquities.* I, even I, am he that *blotteth out thy transgressions for mine own sake, and will not remember thy sins.* PUT ME IN REMEMBRANCE; *let us plead together : declare thou, that thou mayest be justified.*" (Isaiah xliii.) And again, " O Israel, return unto the Lord thy God ; for thou hast fallen by thine iniquity." " I will *heal their backsliding, I will love them freely*; for mine anger is turned away from him. I will be as *the dew unto Israel :* he shall *grow as the lily, and cast forth his roots as Lebanon.*" (Hosea xiv.) " Return, ye backsliding children, and I will heal your backsliding." (Jer. iii. 22.) Our limits preclude our proceeding with quotations, but every one who knows his Bible is well aware of the fact, that similar passages might be greatly multiplied, and that the language of God is ever the same to a transgressor and breaker of His covenant in His ancient Church, if he will only return :—" let him *return* to the Lord, and he will have mercy upon him, and unto our God, *for he will abundantly pardon.*"

We thus see that in the Jewish Church those who had left the covenant of God and become transgressors of the deepest die, were freely invited to return with the assurance that every stain should be washed out, and that they should be viewed by God pure as the unsullied snow. And is it different under the Gospel dispensation? God forbid. It is a melancholy and humiliating spectacle to perceive such misconceptions and perversions of the grace of Christ, so dishonouring to God and so ruinous to man, taught by men of talent, learning, and character, and moreover professing the Protestant faith. It only, however, affords a fresh illustration of that scriptural truth, which we are too apt to forget in our admiration of human prowess and accomplishments, that it is not the wisdom or learning of men that will open to them the riches of the treasures of God. " Ye see your calling, brethren, how that not many wise men after the flesh," &c. " Hath not God made foolish the wisdom of this world ?" " He turneth wise men backward and maketh their knowledge foolish."

Our compassionate Saviour saith—" He that cometh unto me I will IN NO WISE cast out." To all such, coming unto God through him, the language of the New Covenant is as follows—words which it might be thought, from the use made of them by our Church, would be engraven on our hearts:—" If we confess our sins, he is "—not merciful—but " *faithful* and *just* to forgive us our sins, and to *cleanse us from all unrighteousness;*" and " if any man sin, we have an advocate with the Father, Jesus Christ the righteous ; and he is the propitiation for our sins :" " and the blood of Jesus Christ his Son cleanseth us from all sin." This is the Gospel which is to be preached to every creature under heaven ; and whoever perverts it, and whoever would forbid us, we now declare, that every humble, contrite sinner is at once entitled to receive those blessed promises and truths, in their plain and obvious meaning, and to appropriate them to himself, in the full assurance that whoever deceives him, God will and must be true to all his declarations. Let him only believe, and he will, in his own experience, realize the full salvation of God.

Truly melancholy is it, we repeat, to see these professed masters in Israel rendering the word of God of none effect. We might have hoped that at least that *comprehensive* and UNIVERSAL invitation of the compassionate Saviour to the " weary and heavy laden " would have been permitted to shed its balm over the broken and disconsolate heart. " Come unto me,* ALL ye that labour and are heavy laden, and I will give you rest." But no ! the Professor doubts, as we have seen, of the propriety of their application, except to those who had never before known Christ, or to his true disciples about to partake of his body and blood. And so again, " God hath set forth Christ Jesus to be a propitiation through faith in his blood, to declare his righteousness for the remission of sins that are past;" that is, says Professor Pusey, for " *the sins of the times of ignorance.*" And as the *virtue* of Christ's blood is in this manner so wofully limited, so is the extent of his *intercession.* " His intercession" is " for sins into which, *through the infirmity of the flesh,* though Christians, we may fall," but the

---

* Professor Pusey has, in quotation, dropped the comprehensive word ALL, no doubt from inadvertence merely.

E

Professor adds, " we have no account in Scripture of any second remission, obliteration, extinction, of all sin, such as is bestowed upon us
' by the one Baptism for the remission of sins.'" (See page 67.)
And our readers would remark that it is the same reason which is
given for depriving those who have fallen (the great mass of the
English nation, in fact) of the consolation afforded by the Saviour in
his address to the " weary and heavy laden "—namely, " having no
fresh " Baptism for the remission of sins to offer, no means of " renewing them to repentance."

Here, indeed, is an exhibition of the consequences of substituting
the sign for the *thing signified* which is altogether appalling, and may
well inspire a holy fear in the breast of every regenerate man of even
appearing to confound, in his mind or in his ministrations, the shadow
with the substance of the Gospel. These men, elaborately and
learnedly doing this, practically deny the virtue of Christ's blood to
wash away sin. The *scarlet* and *crimson* sins of the fallen, under the
Jewish dispensation, were made *white as snow* through the virtue of
the blood of Him who was to come. But Christ having come, the
minister of a better covenant, established on better promises, in virtue
of which he is able to save them to the uttermost that come unto God
through him, is by such teaching shorn of his glory and robbed of his
power, and poor sinners are well nigh wholly cast out of the reach of
his pardoning mercy, and restoring, comforting, and establishing
grace !

The final issue, then, of the system of teaching of the Oxford divines,
which we have been discussing, is simply this,—to exhibit, on the one
hand, the whole Protestant world who are not in the Holy Apostolic
line, as lying without the bounds of God's covenanted mercies; and
on the other, the entire members of the Popish and regular Evangelical communities, as regenerated and made the children of God in
a higher sense than were Noah, Daniel, and Job; and yet, with comparatively very few exceptions, as having apostatised from the faith,
and consequently lying, as *Apostates*, in a far more hopeless state than
ever did the Jewish and Israelitish Churches, under their most
dreadful departures from their heavenly King. Teaching ending in
such results cannot come from God.

One cannot but remark, in closing this part of the subject, upon the
ignorance of the essential principles of the Gospel displayed by our
Oxford brethren in the view which they take of the method by which
they consider, peradventure, the fallen may be restored. Not to take
into our view the much disputed question of the sin against the Holy
Ghost, they do not seem to perceive that God is infinitely willing, in the

Son of his love, to receive every fallen sinner, and that in every case of a sinner being brought home to God, there is only one way, namely, through a belief in, and appropriation by the sinner, of the blood and righteousness of Christ. Whatever distinction in the character and malignity of the sins of men, in respect of the method of their acceptance with God "there is no difference." *In no case* has the sinner anything to give. He is invited to receive the "free gift." In every case the difficulty is not with God, but in the sinner. And when the latter "is made willing," he finds God, according to his promise, *Gracious*, and that in "the Lord he has righteousness and strength"— *righteousness*, to cover all his unrighteousness—*strength*, to supply all his weakness. The notion quoted with approbation by Professor Pusey, and which is that indeed which gives vitality to *their* whole system of tears and repentance, namely, *that* given expression to in these words, "For how great tears shall we bring before God, that we may equal the fountain of Baptism?" (see page 68)—that is, "having once by Baptism been made 'the child of God,' and having fallen, 'how shall I multiply my tears before Him so as to give them the efficacy and power of Baptism,"—what is this but putting tears in the place of Christ, and making them our Saviour?

We trust our readers now see distinctly that this system of the Oxford divines not only excludes from the covenanted grace of the Gospel all such as "follow not with them," but that it deprives even their own followers of "the glad tidings of great joy," which it is the desire and command of God should be freely dispensed to every creature;—every one being entreated to accept of them freely "without money and without price." We fully agree with the learned Professor that "*until we lay deeper the foundations of repentance, the very preaching of the cross of Christ becomes but the means of carnal security.*" (Page 62.) But he will never lay deep or aright the foundations of Gospel repentance on his present system. It is the way human wisdom may point out, but it is not God's way. God's way is to preach Christ as the full and complete Saviour for sinners of every kind, and in every state and condition—to preach that "He is exalted a Prince and Saviour to *give repentance to Israel and the remission of sins*." The objection that this doctrine leads to licentiousness was urged against and combated by St. Paul, and the objection has never died away from his day to ours. That the grace of the Gospel was abused in his day, and is so in ours, and probably ever will be, we fully admit. There is no truth, no grace, no privilege, which has not been so abused and perverted. But making the fullest admissions of this kind that can be made consistently with verity, still the grand truth remains untouched, that the simple preaching of the cross of Christ—of a full salvation purchased in all its parts by the infinite and most undeserved compassion and love of an Almighty Saviour, is the only effectual means used by the Spirit of God, for breaking in pieces the hard and stony heart of man—of making him to feel in the depths of his heart, the infinite malignity and turpitude of sin in every shape and of every degree, and of enabling him to perceive, that while there is a virtue in the blood, and righteousness, and intercession of his Lord, which is altogether infinite, and which, therefore, changes the crimson of his sins into the purity of the snow, fixes, at the same time, on his regenerated heart, such a deep and abiding impression of the exceeding sinfulness of sin, as no other instrument can accomplish, while it impresses on him by the most moving considerations, his duty and privilege of hating even the " garment spotted with the flesh," and of " perfecting holiness in the fear of the Lord."

The system which we have been considering, in short, though it professes to be the Gospel, is not the Gospel. It is somewhat varnished over and mystified, but in reality it is nothing more than " Do this, and thou shalt live." With Rome, it gives a starting point from Christ, but having done so, it leaves the grace of the Gospel equally with the Papists. Let our readers consider the cruel bondage, brightened with but a few rays of hope, in which Professor Pusey, with the assistance of Tertullian, Hermas, Theodoret, and the other Fathers, places well-nigh the entire population of these Islands. They are to labour, and pray, and fast, and weep, till they work out for themselves a second regeneration. Were they so to labour to all eternity, they would never accomplish it. But whether they labour in joy, or whether they labour in sorrow, labouring on this principle is not according to the Gospel. " To him that *worketh* is the reward *not reckoned of grace* but *of debt*. But to him that *worketh not*, but *believeth* on him that *justifieth* the ungodly, his *faith is counted for righteousness*." (Rom. iv. 4.) In every situation in which a sinner can be placed, his *first* duty—and the more dark and desperate his state, the more urgent the duty—is to come instantly to Christ—to Him who will " *in no wise cast out him* who humbly comes to him." " *This is the work of God*," says the divine Saviour, the beginning and end of it, that which includes every thing else, " *that ye believe on Him whom He hath sent*." It is this coming to Christ, believing that even such a rebel as he will be received—the good hope, the joyful persuasion, that he is received, which breaks the heart of stone which nothing else could break—which makes the tears of godly sorrow and true repentance to flow—which enables him to receive the " word (of salvation) in much affliction," but, also, "with joy in the Holy Ghost." (1 Thess. i. 6.) He derives life from Christ. He is born of the Spirit. And the actings of the new spiritual life are not *to obtain life,* but proceed *from the possession of life.* They are not in exercise to propitiate God, for God is already reconciled to him in the only way it is possible he should be, through the sacrifice and intercession of his Son; but he works from love to God, from the feelings which a son has to his father, and in that state of mind alone in which the obedience of a son can be wholly acceptable to his father. Here is not the toilsome labours of the slave, working amidst sorrow and despondency, if, peradventure, he may propitiate a hard master, but the joyful obedience of a son to a father whom he has most deeply offended, but by whom he has been most freely pardoned, and whom he now, in all humility and self-abasement, but with all joy and thankfulness, reveres, honours, and loves.

We all know that much infirmity, and pain, and sorrow, arising from the weakness and imperfection of their faith, mark the walk even of the most advanced of the saints of God. But this way which we have now pointed out is the way of the Gospel, in opposition to the way of nature; and O that our Oxford brethren, and all who think with them, would be persuaded to believe the testimony of thousands of honest and honourable witnesses who once stood on their ground, but now stand on that which we have now pointed out, when they tell them, that *having tried both,* they find the one as superior to the other, as the way of grace is to the way of nature, and as the wisdom of God rises above and beyond the folly of man.

CHAPTER VII.

BAPTISMAL REGENERATION.—SENTIMENTS OF THE EARLY FATHERS.

WE now proceed, according to our promise, to bring before our readers the sentiments of the early Church on the subject of *Baptismal Regeneration:* and our prefatory observation on the subject is this,— that any man who seriously wishes to have the much-agitated question of Baptismal Regeneration set at rest, would carefully abstain from any reference to the Primitive Church on the subject. We have an unerring standard to which we may appeal; and that standard speaks with no ambiguous or uncertain voice. Members of the Established Church may also appeal to the standards of that Church. And if the information derived from these two sources leave the matter still doubtful, we really cannot see on what ground the hope can be entertained, that it can, by any imaginable possibility, be settled by a reference to the Primitive Church. That reference, however, is now forced upon us by the very confident appeals made to it by the supporters of Baptismal Regeneration; and we are aware that there are some, perhaps many, who are by no means favourable to the doctrine, who are staggered by the confidence of those appeals, and who feel no small uneasiness at the thought of entertaining, on so important a subject, an opinion directly opposed to that held by the immediate successors of the apostles. To that tribunal, therefore, we are compelled, though most reluctantly, to refer the decision of the question. Our reluctance arises from no doubt that we entertain as to what the decision will be, but simply from the fact, that we are called upon to plead before a tribunal to which the question ought never to have been referred.

The question ought never to have been referred to that tribunal, because that tribunal has no authority whatever, nor are we bound to follow it further than it followed the Lord and his apostles. That is, when we adopt any opinion or practice of that Church, we adopt them not because we find them in that Church, but because we find them where no doubt it found them, in holy Scripture. And we are bound to be the more cautious on this point, when we reflect that even in the Apostolic age the mystery of iniquity was at work,—that there were many antichrists,—and that practical errors of serious magnitude had been introduced into the Church. Should a case occur in which the language of Scripture is ambiguous, and the practice of the Primitive Church clear and undoubted, we would, in such a case, hold the practice of the Church to afford the best interpretation of Scripture. But we really cannot at the moment recollect any such case; and it would plainly be a serious imputation upon the sufficiency of Scripture, if a case of the kind could occur, that involved any important principle. Where other evidence is wanting, we will readily receive that of the Primitive Church. But where, as in the present case, we have clear and abundant Scripture evidence, an appeal to that Church is quite superfluous. Nor do even those who most frequently appeal to that Church, in reality allow it any more authority than we do. They are willing to get its support in favour of their views; but when it opposes these views they set aside its authority without the slightest scruple, nor feel that they are guilty of any crime in so doing. Even supposing, therefore, that the Primitive Church should be found to decide the present question in favour of our opponents, upon what possible ground can they call upon us to submit to an authority by which they themselves refuse to be bound?

But supposing the authority of the Primitive Church to be decisive, the question is, how are we to get at its decision? Has it spoken upon the subject so much more clearly than the Scriptures, and our own Articles, as to leave no doubt upon the subject? Every one knows that this is very far from being the case, and that, in point of fact, it were easier to settle the question without reference to the Primitive Church, than to decide what opinion it held upon the subject. To seek for the decision of the question there, is truly to seek for light in the midst of darkness. That they who find Baptismal Regeneration in Scripture, and in our own Articles, will find it also in the Primitive Church, is sufficiently clear, for to us it appears they are prepared to find it any where. But we, on the contrary, maintain that the Primitive Church renounced that doctrine; and we maintain this upon grounds which we shall at least be curious to see how the advocates of that doctrine will contrive to remove.

There are few opinions, and few practices of the Primitive Church, which are not the subjects of dispute; and hence, in general, the impropriety of an appeal to it on any controverted point, since such an appeal is commonly nothing else than an attempt to settle one controversy through the medium of another of still more difficult adjustment. There is, however, one practice of that Church which seems liable to no dispute, and which appears to us to furnish a distinct proof that by it Baptismal Regeneration not only was not held, but was expressly renounced. We refer to the manner in which converts from heretical sects were received. If the Church held the doctrine of Baptismal Regeneration, then the rebaptization of converted heretics became a matter of plain duty and necessity. The Baptism which they had received from the hands of heretics was no Baptism, and could confer no regeneration, nor any spiritual gift. Here, then, was a case which brought the question of Baptismal Regeneration to a clear and distinct issue. A person who has been baptized in some heretical sect applies for admission into the Catholic Church. Does that Church hold the doctrine of Baptismal Regeneration? Then its duty in this case is perfectly plain. The heretical Baptism which this person has received was no Baptism. To admit this would be to admit that the heretical sect had valid ordinances; in other words, were no heretics, but a true Church. But could an unregenerated person be admitted? That was impossible. The

Church, then, had no alternative. The applicant was unregenerated. By Baptism alone could that Regeneration be conferred. Of necessity, therefore, he must be baptized.

Did the Church, then, acknowledge this necessity, and rebaptize the applicant? It did not. It thus distinctly declared, either that Regeneration was unnecessary,—a declaration which, we need hardly say, it never could make; or that Regeneration might be possessed without any Baptism, excepting that which was communicated by men who had not, nor pretended to have, any *Apostolical Succession.*

Nor can it be said that the Church in this case acted from mere inadvertency. The matter was, at an early period, brought very prominently into view by Cyprian, who, holding the doctrine of Baptismal Regeneration—though not, we suspect, in a sense that will afford the modern advocates of that doctrine much support—consistently urged the rebaptization of all heretics on their reception into the Church. He would not, indeed, allow it to be called *re*baptizing, but only baptizing, holding that the baptism which they had previously received was no Baptism. And, granting the doctrine of Baptismal Regeneration to be true, there seems to be no possible way of either resisting or evading so plain and undeniable a conclusion.

But did the Church take this view of the matter? No: Cyprian stood alone. The Church was unanimously and universally, in principle and in practice, opposed to his view of the matter. He wrote much, and he wrote earnestly; and, on the supposition that Baptismal Regeneration was the doctrine of the Church, he wrote resistlessly. Nay, on this supposition, he could have met with no resistance. He was maintaining what we are gravely and solemnly told was the faith of the Church at that time. Yet he wrote in vain! The Church refused to rebaptize converted heretics, thus plainly declaring that it did not consider Baptism, administered by the hands of men deriving their commission from the regular Apostolical Succession, to be necessary to Regeneration.

In fact, we hear of no rebaptizing in the Church till the fourth century, when the Council of Nice ordained that converted Paulianists should be baptized; and nearly half a century later, the Council of Laodicea made the same order with regard to the Montanists. And both these decrees rested upon special reasons, and applied only to the sects named. Nay, we find Gregory, Bishop of Rome, in the fifth century, ordaining that no man should be rebaptized who recollected that he had been baptized, though he could not recollect in what sect he had received Baptism. Such was the respect paid by the Primitive Church to the Apostolical Succession, and to the necessary connexion of Regeneration with Baptism conferred by Apostolical men.

Now, taking for our guide the Primitive Church, to which an appeal is so often made, we would ask the Oxford divines how we can possibly contrive, in the face of these facts, to adopt their sentiments? The facts themselves, we suppose, they will not attempt to deny. How then do they account for them? Did the Primitive Church deny the necessity of Regeneration? That they will not say. Did that Church hold that the Baptism of excommunicated heretics and schismatics could confer Regeneration? To admit that would be utterly to ruin their whole system. We beg them to instruct us then, for we are unable even to conjecture how they can account for the practice of that Church which stands in such direct and irreconcileable opposition to the sentiments which they ascribe to it. In the meantime, we hope our readers will be disposed to believe that the principles and the practice of the Primitive Church were in harmony with one another; and that the writers who have called forth these remarks, have, in their haste to find authority for their own opinions, naturally fallen into the mistake of attributing to that Church sentiments which it never held—sentiments which that Church plainly renounced in practice, and never, so far as we know, held in theory.

In proceeding to bring under the view of our readers the opinions of some of the most eminent of the early Fathers on the subject, we find that our contracted limits will greatly confine us in regard to the number of those to whom we so refer. We simply state, however, that our knowledge of the Fathers is far from being limited to those from whose writings we shall quote; and we ask credit from our readers when we affirm, that if the impression conveyed to them in respect of this subject from the writers from whom we shall now quote, stultifies the opinions of our Oxford brethren, a fair and intelligent reference to the entire works of the early Fathers which have reached us, would produce the same just impression. In prosecuting our work we beg to recal to the recollection of our readers a distinction which we made in a previous chapter, between the practice of the Primitive Church, and the sentiments of primitive writers. This distinction is of the utmost importance; so much so, indeed, that if every writer whose works have come down to us held the doctrine of Baptismal Regeneration, we must still hold, on the evidence just produced, that that was not the doctrine of the Church. To illustrate this, let us suppose that a thousand years hence it should be maintained, that in the nineteenth century the Church of England held the doctrine of Baptismal Regeneration. And to render the proof of this as strong as possible, let us farther suppose that the writings of those who oppose that doctrine have perished, while the works of those who maintain it remain; that such ephemeral publications as the present are extinct, and other works of a more permanent character maintaining similar views have likewise perished, but that the Oxford Tracts are extant, and attended too with all the weight which they can derive from having been produced in the most celebrated seat of learning in the kingdom. Here he who maintains this to have been the doctrine of the Church of England in the nineteenth century has every advantage. Yet what would these advantages avail him, if at the same time it could be proved, that during that century, the Church of England, throughout the whole of her parishes, received freely converts from every sect without baptizing them; and moreover, in her funeral service, declared even those Dissenters who had never entered her communion to be baptized persons? It would plainly be useless to quote the Oxford Tracts, or any similar writings. This could only prove the sentiments of the writers; but never could, in direct opposition to her own practice, prove that such sentiments formed any part of the creed of the English Church.

This argument would become not more conclusive, but more striking, if it could be proved that the very men who wrote most keenly in support of Baptismal Regeneration, were themselves ministers in the Church of England, and did, in discharging the duties of that sacred office, declare the Baptism of Dissenters to be good and valid Baptism, at the very time that they were in their writings declaring that they in reality held it to be a nullity. It is no violent or improbable supposition to suppose, that in the congregations of some of the writers whom we are opposing, there may be individuals who have no other Baptism than that which they received in some Dissenting community. Now how do they deal with those individuals? If they admit them to the participation of the Christian ordinances, they are obviously, on their own principles, casting that which is holy to dogs; they are introducing to the Lord's house and to the Lord's table those who have never " entered in by the door," but who are " strangers to the covenants of promise, without God, and without hope in the world;" and they are giving a false peace, as if they were children of God, to men who they believe will ultimately be cast out as unregenerated, from the presence of the Lord. How men can for a single day continue to be the ministers of a Church in which they find themselves obliged to act in a manner so opposite to their declared convictions, we cannot tell. This, however, is matter for their own consciences, with which we shall not intermeddle.

From these illustrations, we trust our readers will see, in the most distinct manner, the force of the argument by which we have proved that the Primitive Church stands clear of the charge of sanctioning the doctrine of Baptismal Regeneration. They will see also the reality and the importance of the distinction which we have drawn between the practice of the Church and the sentiments of individual writers. They will see that though the whole of those writers should maintain that doctrine, their maintenance of it will not prove that the Church held it. But we suppose our readers are by this time beginning to think that these remarks are intended also for the farther purpose of introducing an admission that the primitive writers do maintain the doctrine of Baptismal Regeneration. They are intended, however, for no such purpose. That admission we could well afford to make, and would make it without hesitation, did truth require it of us. But truth makes no such demand. The primitive writers speak so loosely and vaguely on this, as on many other subjects, as to render it a matter of no small difficulty to determine exactly what they teach with regard to it. And certainly he who undertakes to prove that they held the doctrine in question, in any sense that can be useful to the present assertors of it, will soon find that he has undertaken a Sysiphean task. But to make our remarks on this part of our subject as distinct as possible, we shall, in the first instance, take a single writer, for the purpose of exemplifying them as we go on. The writer whom we choose for this purpose is Tertullian. We choose him because he has written a treatise on Baptism; because he assigns his reasons, such as they are, for the opinions which he holds; and because he is one of the writers particularly selected by our Oxford brethren, and often and confidently appealed to in support of the opinions which we oppose.

In his treatise, Tertullian certainly speaks of Baptism in the loftiest terms, of which the reader has had, already, abundant evidence. It washes away our sins; it removes our guilt and our punishment; it gives us eternal life. It occurs to him, however, that people may wonder that so simple a matter as water should produce such splendid effects. He therefore proceeds to show the grounds on which he holds water to possess such extraordinary power. These reasons are, that water is the oldest and purest of the elements; that it is the most dignified, since God chose it for His seat when the Spirit brooded over the deep; that God employed it as His instrument in arranging the world; that it was the first element which produced living things;

that it entered into the original composition of man, who was indeed made of earth, but not dry and sapless earth, which would have been unfit for the purpose, but earth moistened with water. No wonder, then, concludes Tertullian, that water in Baptism should have the power of conferring life—" *Ne mirum sit in baptismo si aquæ animare noverunt.*"

Now what is the weight of Tertullian's authority in this case? The stream cannot rise higher than the fountain, and his authority can hardly be of greater weight than the reasons on which it is avowedly founded. Had he assigned no reason for his opinion, we might have supposed that he had really some good reasons for it. But when he has given us reasons which the gravest of Oxford's professors can hardly read with gravity, and which the youngest of her students would spurn with contempt, if seriously addressed to him, we would ask, is it decent, is it fair, that we should be borne down with the weight of his authority, while the very men who quote it would hold it an insult to be supposed capable of attaching the slightest weight to his arguments? Is it honourable thus to influence the modest and the ignorant, by the authority of a man whose reasons, if produced, would deprive his authority of all weight?

But after all, does Tertullian really sanction the opinions of those who quote him? Does he hold that by Baptism we are made partakers of the Spirit? He does not. For after five chapters in praise of water, he opens the sixth with the startling and unexpected declaration, " Not that in the water we receive the Holy Spirit, but that, cleansed in the water, we are, under the angel, prepared for the Holy Spirit." " *Non quod in aquis Spiritum sanctum consequamur, sed in aqua emundati, sub angelo Spiritui Sancto proparamur.*" The fact is, that as the Lord had a forerunner, he holds it necessary that the Holy Spirit should have one too. He, therefore, introduces an angel, whom he calls *Baptismi Arbiter*, who alone is present at the Baptism with water, and prepares us thereby for the Spirit. The gift of the Spirit, if connected with any ceremony, is given by means of the Chrism. Nor did Tertullian stand alone in this opinion. Is this the opinion of the present asserters of Baptismal Regeneration? Do they hold that it is not by the water, but by the Chrism, that we are made partakers of the Spirit? If not, then what weight do they attach to Tertullian's authority? or how can they call upon us to submit to an authority by which they themselves refuse to be bound? That part of his opinions which they adopt, rests upon no higher authority, nor is supported by better reasons than that which they reject. Where is the consistency of this? We need hardly remark that our Church has rejected the Chrism, as an unscriptural addition to the ordinance of Baptism, and has thus removed the grand foundation on which the doctrine of Baptismal Regeneration rested; and the present assertors of that doctrine differ alike widely from the Primitive Church, and from the Church of England. In so doing Tertullian lends them not the slightest support. He held, it is true, the doctrine for which they plead; but he founded his opinion on reasons which they would be ashamed to produce,—he attributed to the ordinance much more than they think proper to say that they attribute to it,—and he attributed its power to regenerate and communicate the Spirit, to a part of the ordinance, which, unless they enter the Church of Rome, they will never have any opportunity of administering, since our own Church has abolished it, and most properly.

Before leaving Tertullian, let us remark, that while he held that, for the sake of *peace and good order*, a clergyman should usually be employed to baptize, it was on this account alone he held the opinion; for he maintained that any man who had been baptized, had as good a right to baptize, and as ample power to confer all the benefits of Baptism, as any clergyman whatever. What say the advocates of Apostolic Succession to this? Will they accept of Tertullian's authority in this case? They will not.

But to proceed. The Fathers commonly speak in such vague and general terms, that it is very difficult to ascertain exactly what they mean. Yet, when amidst their vague generalities we do get a glimpse of their exact opinions, we often find them more correct than we should have anticipated. Thus Clement of Alexandria is often referred to by the supporters of Baptismal Regeneration; and he certainly speaks of it as they would wish. Yet in one place (Strom. v. 2) he says that among Christians, " to teach and enlighten is called to regenerate." Το καταχησαι τι και φωτισαι, αναγεννησαι λεγεται. This is an opinion which a believer in Baptismal Regeneration cannot hold. In the Bishop of Oxford's edition of Clement, the Note on this expression, whether written by the Bishop himself or selected, he does not say, concludes in this manner,—*Nota, quod illuminatio baptismum præcedat. Est tamen hæc vox pro ipso baptismo sæpe usurpata.* Yes, Baptism is often called illumination, but it is the sign of an illumination which comes from a different source. In the same way, by a very natural metonymy, it is called Regeneration. Nor can we wonder that such terms should be applied to it, when we consider the care that was taken, and the evidence that was required, that the candidate for Baptism was truly an enlightened and regenerated person. Besides, the Fathers, especially the earliest of them, wrote carelessly, because they did not expect that any improper conclusions would be drawn from the looseness of their language. So it is, however, that there are few errors which may not be sanctioned by some of their expressions.

If, however, we must rigidly interpret the language of the Fathers, we must say, that the doctrine which they held was not Baptismal Regeneration, but Chrismal Regeneration. Baptism with water they considered as only a preparation for Baptism with the Holy Spirit, which latter was communicated by anointing with oil, and the imposition of hands. This we have seen was Tertullian's opinion, who distinctly says that it is not in the water that we receive the Spirit, but that the angel, the *Baptismal Arbiter,* by it prepares us for the Spirit. It is unnecessary to make any quotations to show that this was the common opinion; but we select a few for the purpose of throwing some farther light on this discussion. In the " Questions to the Orthodox," attributed to Justin, Question 14, it is asked how the Church can be blameless in admitting converted heretics without baptizing them, since their Baptism is false and vain, and also in acknowledging the orders of such of them as have been ordained? The reply is, that every thing heretical about them is corrected; their heretical sentiments, by their change of opinion; their Baptism, by the holy unction; and their ordination, by the imposition of hands; so that whatever previously belonged to them is abolished. Here we see that heretical Baptism was held valid; but not heretical Chrism. Baptism with water they could confer, though no true Church; but not Baptism with the Holy Spirit, whom they had not, and could not give. Here too, it is plain that Regeneration is not connected with Baptism with water, unless our opponents will maintain that men may be regenerated without the Holy Spirit, which we suppose they will hardly do, but with the Chrism, which was the Baptism with the Holy Spirit.

We come next to the author of the tract against Cyprian's views on the Baptism of heretics, and which is appended to that Father's works. We take from him the following sentence :—" *Multum interest utrum in totum quis non sit baptizatus in nomine Domini nostri Jesu Christi, an vero in aliquo claudicet cum baptizatur baptismate aquæ, quod minus est, dummodo postea constet in veritate sincera fidei in baptismate Spiritus, quod majus est.*" Here we have the difference between Baptism by water, and Baptism by the Spirit, as plain as language can make it, and the superior importance of the latter stated. In the correctness of this notion our readers may, perhaps, be disposed to

acquiesce. But they will see better what the author means when we
have quoted another sentence about two pages further on. He there
says,—" *Et ideo cum Salus nostra in baptismate Spiritus, quod plerumque
cum baptismate aquæ conjunctum est, sit constituta, si quidem per nos bap-
tisma tradetur, integre et Sollemniter et per omnia quæ, scripta sunt
adsignetur, atque sine ulla ullius rei separatione tradatur : aut si a minore
clero per necessitatem traditum fuerit, eventum expectemus, ut aut suppleatur
a nobis, aut a Domino supplendum reservetur. Si vero ab alienis traditum
fuerit, ut potest hoc negotium, et ut admittit, corrigatur.*" Here we are
told that Baptism by the Spirit, *for the most part*, accompanied the
Baptism with water. In fact, when first introduced, the Chrism and
imposition of hands formed only an appendage to Baptism, and constituted a part of the ceremony. And the practice of keeping them
united seems, *for the most part*, to have prevailed still. This writer,
however, argues that there is no necessity for uniting them. The
Baptism of the Spirit may be communicated at any distance of time
after the Baptism by water. And immediately before the first of the
above quoted passages, he cites the case of the Apostles, who had all
received Baptism by water before the Lord's death. But they had
then only what he calls a *scabra fides*—there was a *lameness* about
them both in faith and in doctrine, as they showed by forsaking the
Lord ; and it was not till the day of Pentecost that they were baptized
with the Spirit and made perfect.

From this, and other examples, he concludes that converted heretics
may receive the Baptism of the Spirit, without renewing the Baptism
by water. The Apostles themselves had neither an entire nor a
perfect faith, *nec integra nec perfecta fides*. Yet they were not
rebaptized, but only baptized with the Spirit.

It will be observed, from the second quotation, that the inferior
clergy baptized only in cases of necessity. The Baptism was not
complete until the bishop had performed his part. Hence to baptize
was his peculiar prerogative: and, therefore, the Baptism of the
Spirit, *for the most part*, accompanied Baptism by water,—because
Baptism was usually performed by the bishop, who could complete the
Baptism : and only in case of necessity, by the inferior clergy, who
could confer only the least important part of it. If a person, baptized
through necessity, by any of the inferior clergy, recovered, the Bishop
then completed the Baptism. If not, then the case was left in the
Lord's own hands. *Eventum expectemus*, says our author : it depends
on the event of his recovery, whether his Baptism shall be completed
on earth or not. Now, it is commonly understood, that at first all
Christians baptized. We have quoted Tertullian's distinct opinion,

that every layman had a right to baptize. And we believe that no Theologian, ancient or modern, whose opinion is worth the asking on the subject, will be found to maintain that Baptism, conferred by a layman, is invalid, and that he who has received it ought to be baptized anew. The practice would introduce ruinous confusion; but the validity of the ordinance so administered, very few, and those of little note, will be found to deny. We may just ask, in passing, if the Oxford brethren are prepared to maintain that the Primitive Church held, and that an immense majority of divines of all ages and of all creeds have held, that every baptized layman has the power of conferring Regeneration?

Our author, however, introduces us into a new state of things. Now, it is only in cases of necessity that any, even of the inferior clergy, can be permitted to baptize. And when they do so, they can confer only Baptism by water, *quod minus est.* The bishop has something to bestow which they cannot give. The appendage to Baptism is now rising into importance, and we see here the germ of what ultimately became an additional Sacrament. Indeed Cyprian distinctly calls it by this name (Epistle 72), where, insisting on the re-baptization of heretics and schismatics, he says they may become the sons of God *si sacramento utroque nascantur*—that is, by Baptism with water, and Baptism with the Holy Spirit.

Before coming to the conclusion to which these quotations and remarks are leading us, it would be unpardonable to pass by Cyprian himself, the great oracle of those who hold Baptismal Regeneration. He stood boldly forward to plead for the legitimate consequences of his opinion that heretical Baptism was no Baptism, namely, that converted heretics should be baptized. He formed a party which gathered many of the African bishops into its bosom, and met with some support in the East. His reasoning appears to be perfectly conclusive. The Church is *one.* Baptism belongs only to the Church, and is also one. There can no more be two true baptisms, than there can be two true Churches. They that have not received the Baptism of the Church, have not received Baptism at all. But an opinion and a practice had by this time sprung up in the Church, which strongly tended to make Cyprian's arguments of no avail. A distinction was now made between Baptism by water, and Baptism by the Holy Spirit. Though the one was as yet, *for the most part*, accompanied with the other, yet it was held that they were different things, and might be separated by any distance of time from one another. And in fact they were, at the time, in the progress of coming to an actual and permanent separation. Now had the Church held that

Baptism with water was attended with Regeneration, then there is obviously no reason why Cyprian's opinion should be resisted; and no ground on which it could be resisted with any hope of success. But Baptism with water, and with the Spirit, were entirely different things. It was enough, therefore, that converted heretics should receive the latter. The former was deemed unnecessary. Hence Cyprian raised his voice in vain. The more so, that he himself distinctly held the opinion which was ruinous to his arguments, namely, that Baptism with water and with the Spirit, were perfectly distinct.

Cyprian, however, is too high an authority with the supporters of the opinion which we oppose, and too important a witness in the matter, to be dismissed without referring to his direct testimony. For this purpose we take his seventieth Epistle. It is too long to be copied here; but there are three points in it to which we would beg the attention of the Oxford writers. First, he denies the validity of heretical Baptism. Next, he asserts the necessity of the Chrism. On this point we give his own words,—*Ungi quoque necesse est cum qui baptizatus sit, ut accepto Chrismate, id est, unctione, esse unctus Dei, et habere in se gratiam Christi possit. Porro autem Eucharistia est unde baptizati unguntur, oleum in altari sanctificatum.* And farther, he argues for the unity of the Church, from the fact that it is founded on Peter.

Now, here are three opinions asserted by the same man, in the same epistle, and that occupying not more than a page. Do the Oxford writers, out of deference to this Father's authority, adopt these three opinions? No; we suppose they will say that two out of the three they entirely repudiate. What weight, then, do they attach to Cyprian's authority? Clearly not the weight of a feather, when it opposes their own views. Can they then hold us guilty of any presumptuous undervaluing of antiquity, when we say that we hold his authority to be as utterly valueless when produced in support of the first of these opinions, as they hold it when produced in support of the other two? If they say that they adopt the first, not because Cyprian held it, but because it is founded on Scripture, we at once agree with them. If it be founded on Scripture, we shall adopt it, even though Cyprian had opposed as strongly as he maintains it. Cyprian's authority is, then, entirely set aside; and if they mean to deal fairly with us, they will quote him no more.

But let us look at the Scripture evidence which he produces in support of his first opinion. He gives the following texts, " They have forsaken me, the fountain of living waters, and have hewed out to themselves broken cisterns, that can hold no water." " Abstain from strange water, and from the fountain of strange water thou shalt not drink." " I will sprinkle clean water upon you, and make you clean," &c.

And then he asks, how can he cleanse and sanctify water, who is himself unclean? when God says, in Numbers, that " whatsoever an unclean person touches shall be unclean." Now if any man can out of these texts extract any doctrine whatever, with regard to Christian Baptism, we may admire his ingenuity, but should hardly think of choosing him for our guide in the exposition of Scripture.

Our readers will now see, that the ordinance of Baptism was gradually divided into two parts, the one of which was held more sacred and important than the other. The Lord announced the necessity of being born of water and of the Spirit. The one of these is understood to be the outward sign and seal of the other. But the ancients soon came to hold them as two different things. The one was of minor importance, and might be conferred and possessed by those who were destitute of the Spirit, and who lived and died in unrepented and unforgiven heresy. Being born by the Spirit had its own peculiar sign, and could be conferred and enjoyed only in the Church. Each of these was called Regeneration—being born again. We have said that Baptism was called Regeneration by a very natural metonymy: our readers will now see another ground on which it was so called. He who was baptized according to the Lord's command, was born of water,—was, in this sense, regenerated. If this be the sense in which the present supporters of the doctrine of Baptismal Regeneration understand the word, we really think it was hardly worth making such a noise about it; since, in this sense, every one who is baptized, whether in the Church or among heretics, is unquestionably born of water, or regenerated. But this sense they will reject as totally unsuitable to their purpose. But if by Regeneration, they mean a spiritual New Birth, such a change as the word is usually understood in modern theology to express, then the very writers whom they summon to their aid renounce them; for these writers attach this privilege to a Baptism, which they do not pretend that they can give.

Whatever sense, then, they attach to the word Regeneration, their appeal to the Primitive Church, and to the early writers, entirely fails them. They meet in these with Baptismal Regeneration, but in no sense that gives them the slightest support. And our readers will now also see the folly of appealing to the early writers. We would ask those who most confidently make that appeal, if they will take any one writer, or all the writers whose authority they adduce, and be bound to adopt all their opinions, or acquiesce in all their reasonings? They will tell us that they will be bound by no such condition. They will tell us that all around, above, and below the sentiments which they quote, lie other sentiments which they utterly reject, and reasonings which they utterly scorn. What good purpose, then, we would ask, can be answered by dragging us to a tribunal, by whose decisions the very men who make the appeal refuse to be bound, and to whose authority they attach as little weight as we can do? We surely make no unreasonable demand, when, we say, either let the authority of the Fathers be openly maintained, so that we may feel satisfied that we are building on a sure foundation when we have their support; or let them be entirely abandoned, and let this, and all other questions be decided by that rule whose authority we all own. As any appeal to them can tend only to perplex a plain question, we shall be exceedingly glad to see them abandoned, and all that we have written on this part of the subject thus rendered superfluous. But if the Fathers must decide the question, then the decision is plainly against our opponents: for—

If by Regeneration they merely mean being born of water, then their pretensions are ridiculous, according to the doctrine of the Primitive Church, which conceded the power of granting this Regeneration to laymen, to heretics, and to schismatics, of every name. This we suppose, they will hardly venture to call in question; and if this be the privilege for which they plead, we should think the time wasted that is spent in contesting it, since a man may have this Regeneration, and yet be spiritually dead and a child of wrath.

If by Regeneration they mean Baptism with the Spirit—spiritual Regeneration—then we think we have sufficiently showed, that, according to the Fathers, that was something entirely different from being born of water, and was by them attached to a Baptism which the Oxford brethren will not pretend that they can bestow.

If, finally, they have, with thousands more, permitted themselves to be misled by the mere ambiguity of a word applied to things so widely different, as being born of water and being born of the Spirit, and thus have received a distorted impression of the doctrine of the Primitive Church, we think the learning of Oxford would have been better employed in correcting, than in deepening such an impression.

CHAPTER VIII.

CONCLUSION.—RECENT CHANGE IN THE PULPIT MINISTRATIONS OF
THE CHURCH OF ENGLAND.

We have now accomplished what we intended in the series of papers on High Church Principles, which we now bring to a close. Without any attempt at recapitulation, we commend the whole to the serious attention of our readers, with the humble, but fervent prayer, that if we have ignorantly advanced any thing in opposition to the word of God, this our sin of ignorance may be forgiven, and that wherein we have written in accordance with the sacred oracles, the truth thus circulated throughout the kingdom may produce its due and legitimate effect.

We have described High Church principles " as those which would lodge power and attribute properties to the visible Church, and especially to the Sacraments as administered by her, beyond and above those with which she is invested by the great Head of the Church, as unfolded in the Scriptures of truth ;" and we illustrated, in our first chapter, the accuracy of this definition by a reference to various doctrines and assumptions of the Papacy.

A reference to the dogmas and pretensions of the High Church party in the Church of England, as presented in the *Oxford Tracts* and the *British Magazine*, and which we have now exhibited to our readers, will, in like manner, prove its accuracy. We have seen that these men, themselves accursed and excommunicated by the Romish Church, adopt language, though more measured, of the like tendency and effect, as is addressed by that apostate community to themselves; and by limiting, in a manner abhorrent to the principles, and set at nought by the practice, of the Fathers of our Church, the power of preaching the Gospel and administering the Sacraments to the members of "the Holy Apostolic line," exalt themselves, and their office, and their powers, beyond the line of Scripture, while they cast all others to the ground. They require us, on the one hand, " to be as sure that the Bishop is Christ's appointed representative, as if we actually saw him work miracles as St. Peter and St. Paul did" (*Oxford Tracts*, Vol. i. No. 10); and on the other, to believe that "a person who ministers in holy things not commissioned from the Bishop, is all the while treading in the footsteps of Korah, Dathan, and Abiram." (*Ibid.*, No. 85.) Thus, in the case of the Papacy, and of this section of our own Church, the like ends are gained, and by like means.

It is our earnest desire and prayer that that part of the Church which is usually denominated Evangelical, may be preserved from the snare laid for their feet by men professing High Church principles. And we beg to assure all such, and especially the younger members of the body, that men, deservedly of the highest name in the Church, who have for many years laboured with distinguished usefulness and honour in her service, and whose judgment, were we authorized to state it, would carry with it the greatest weight, look with deep alarm at this deliberate and zealous attempt to remove them from the simplicity of the faith, and to innoculate them with a *virus* essentially deadly in its nature, and destructive in its consequences.

It is, with all reverence be it spoken, God the Spirit who has accomplished the vast change which has been effected in our Church within the last fifty years. What a minute seed was the Gospel, preached in simplicity, in this country, in the early days of Romaine, Venn, Milner, Berridge, and other such worthies. How were their names cast out as evil, and their principles viewed as utterly fanatical and visionary. What a change even, since the Rev. Mr. Simeon was repeatedly black-balled in the Bartlett's-buildings Society, as utterly unworthy of a place in that centre of Orthodoxy, and now that men of his principles are freely admitted by hundreds, and the light of Divine truth which they promulgate is contending, even in that sphere, against the darkness of error. The change is vast. It forces the exclamation from the lips of the intelligent observer, "What has God wrought!" and the prayer from his heart, that the dawn of the morning may only give place to the perfect day.

But the tactics of the enemy appear to be changed, and accommodated, like those of an able general, to the altered and unexpected circumstances in which he finds himself placed. Openly to oppose, brow-beat, and vilify, as in former times, a section of the Church composed of thousands of the most orthodox, diligent, faithful, successful, and influential of the clergy, is now perceived to be a hopeless, and at the same time a perilous task. Peace, *in public*, is, for the most part, declared. The representation has been diligently circulated that, in doctrine, there is no material difference or distinction between those two well-understood and well-defined parties;

and we have good reason to know, that the attempt has been for long systematically carried forward by certain influential parties in the Church, to reduce the *doctrinal* views of the Evangelical clergy to the High Church level (as now fixed), and to bring up the High Church *practice* to the standard of Evangelical zeal and diligence. The attempt of the Oxford divines may be considered to be an independent effort, operating, however, to the same end—to increase the diligence of the clergy, but to make it spring from a different and distinct root from that from which has germinated all the zeal and effective ministration which we see in our Church in the present day, and from which alone any truly saving operation can distinguish any Church in any age. The Gospel method which has been successful among ourselves, and can alone be successful in any Church and at any time, is to preach Christ, in all simplicity and fulness, as the friend and Saviour of sinners. The Oxford method may be most easily distinguished from this by that characteristic direction to the young minister, to " preach the Sacraments."

Now, it is against this attempt, however well intended, that we are especially desirous of warning our younger brethren in the ministry. That such as we are friends of contention and war, and disposed to stir up hostility amongst those who ought to live together in love, is a favourite allegation against us, made especially by those who are working for the accomplishment of the union which we deprecate. It is false and injurious. We desire to contend to the death for the truth. But it is for THE TRUTH. To be " valiant for the truth " we consider one of the first duties and highest honours of man ; and to let a love of peace, or a regard to the interests of any particular community, or any subsidiary consideration whatever, interfere with our zeal for the vindication of the truth, and our defence of it when threatened with contamination, we judge the essence of unfaithfulness and dishonour. We desire to " follow peace with all men," but it is peace founded upon an acknowledgment and vindication of " the truth," not resting upon and cemented by its sacrifice.

It is a remarkable peculiarity connected with this disposition and endeavour to reduce all the clergy to one doctrinal level, that those most desirous of its attainment, systematically and most sedulously refrain from the acknowledgment that any doctrinal change was needed, or indeed has occurred in the Church. It is, in truth, amusing to perceive the care with which the acknowledgment is avoided—so carefully, that it would appear the abstinence arose from a disbelief of any having taken place. It will be well, therefore, to glance for a moment at what that change really is. If we lose sight of the change we shall cease to be conscious of its magnitude, or to appreciate the infinite value of the simple instrumentality by which the mighty work has, so far, been accomplished.

The change consists of two parts—*first*, of the introduction of the simple preaching of the cross of Christ, by which alone a radically religious and moral change can be effected in the hearts and lives of the hearers, and the soul, in consequence, be saved ; and, *secondly*, of a drawing up of the doctrinal views and preaching of the *High Church* to a higher level than that on which they reposed before the wide establishment of the simple preaching of the Gospel. No statement is more offensive and irritating to a genuine High Churchman than this. Yet it is most true, and, though it is nearly unnecessary, we shall afford some evidence of its truth.

Bishop Horsley must be accounted no partial or inadequate judge in a case of this kind. The greater part of a charge to his clergy, delivered in 1790, is occupied with an exposition of the general departure which at that period existed from the preaching of the Gospel. In this charge the following passages occur :—

" Erroneous maxims are gone abroad, which, for several years past, if my observation deceive me not, have very much *governed* the conduct of the *parochial clergy* in the *ministration of the Word.*"— (*Charge*, 1790, p. 3.) These maxims, he tells us, are " That it is more the office of a Christian teacher, to press the *practice* of religion upon the consciences of his hearers, than to inculcate and assert its *doctrines.*" And " That *practical religion and morality* are *one* and the *same thing :* That *moral duties* constitute the whole, or by far the better part of *practical Christianity.*"—(*Ibid.*, pp. 4, 5.) " Both these maxims," his Lordship proceeds, " are erroneous : Both, as far as they are received, have a pernicious influence on the ministry of the word. The first, most absurdly separates practice from the motives of practice. The second, adopting that separation, reduces practical Christianity to heathen virtue ; and the two taken together have much contributed to *divest our sermons of the genuine spirit and labours of Christianity*, AND TO REDUCE THEM TO MERE MORAL ESSAYS. The system chiefly in request with those who seem most in earnest in this strain of preaching, is the strict, but impracticable, unsocial, sullen morality of the *Stoics.* Thus under the influence of these two pernicious maxims, it too often happens, that we *lose sight of that which is our proper office*, to publish the word of reconciliation, to propound the terms of peace and pardon to the penitent ; and *we make no other use of the high commission that we bear, than to come abroad one day in the seven ; dressed in solemn looks, and in the external garb of holiness, to be the* APES OF EPICTETUS."—(*Ibid.*, pp. 5, 6.)

This, we think, is pretty decisive evidence.

In a *Charge* of *Bishop Horne*, delivered in the year 1792, the following passage occurs :—

" Of late times there hath been a prejudice in favour of good *moral preaching,* as if the people might do *very well,* or even *better* without the knowledge of the Christian mysteries ; a good moral life being the end of all teaching. The enemies of Christianity, taking advantage of this prejudice, have made a total separation between the works of religion and its doctrines, pleading the example and authority of some of our divines. And it *must not be concealed,* that by delivering cold *inanimate lectures on moral virtue, independent of Christianity,* MANY OF OUR CLERGY *of late years* have lost themselves very much in the estimation of the religious part of the laity."—(P. 14.)

Where shall we find a man whose judgment in such matters is more entitled to consideration than Archbishop Secker ? In *Charge* I., p. 79, Watson's Tracts, Vol. vi., the following passages occur :—

" To improve the people effectually, . . . you must be assiduous in teaching the principles, not only of virtue and natural religion, but of THE GOSPEL ; and of the Gospel, not as ALMOST EXPLAINED AWAY by modern refiners, but as the truth is in Jesus ; as it is taught by the Church of which you are members ; as you have engaged by your subscriptions and declarations that you will teach it yourselves. You must preach to them faith in the ever-blessed Trinity ; . . . you must set forth the original corruption of our nature ; our redemption, according to God's eternal purpose in Christ, by the Sacrifice of the cross ; our sanctification by the influences of the Divine Spirit ; the insufficiency of good works, and the efficacy of faith to salvation. . . . .

" The *truth,* I fear, is, that MANY, IF NOT MOST OF US, have dwelt too little on these doctrines in our sermons, . . . partly from not having studied theology deeply enough to treat of them ably and efficiently ; God grant it may never have been for want of inwardly experiencing their importance ! But, whatever be the cause, *the effect has been lamentable—our people have grown less and less mindful, first of the distinguishing* articles of their·creed, *then,* as will always be the case, *of that one which they hold in common with the heathens ;* . . . flattering themselves that what they are pleased to call a moral and harmless life, though far from being either, is the one thing needful. . . . Reflections have been made upon us . . . on account of these things, by Deists, Papists, brethren of our own," &c.

And once more, *Bishop Porteus* thus expresses himself in his *Charge,* 1799, pp. 22, 23 :—

" More particularly, it will not be sufficient to *amuse your hearers* with *ingenious moral essays* on the dignity of human nature, the beauty of virtue, and the deformity and inconvenience of vice. This will be a feeble and ineffectual effort, will be as sounding brass and tinkling cymbal. If you wish for any effectual success you must take a very different course. You must lay before your people, with plainness and with force, the great *fundamental doctrines* of the Gospel ;" and having enumerated them, " These," his Lordship proceeds, " are the great Evangelical doctrines which must be pressed repeatedly, with devout and solemn earnestness, on the minds of your hearers, which can alone speak to their consciences, their affections, and their hearts."

That such men as these, occupying situations so distinguished and responsible, speaking officially, in the presence of the Church's enemies, should express themselves with such distinctness, with so little reserve and circumlocution, shows plainly the frightful height to which the evil must have attained, and the great deliverance which we have since then experienced. The sermons in those days, it would appear, upon the authority of Bishop Horsley, were reduced " to mere moral essays:" and so great and notorious was the evil, that he considered himself bound officially and publicly to state, that the clergy, generally, had lost sight of " *their proper office*," and used " the high commission that they bore," " to come abroad one day in the seven, dressed in solemn looks, and in the external garb of holiness, to be the APES of EPICTETUS." And so far from this being deemed an exaggerated, unnecessary, or unbecoming representation of the state of the case, that *Bishop Horne*, two years afterwards, with a particular reference to this *Charge* of Bishop Horsley (as a note informs us) says :—" And as *the unedefying morality of our pulpits* is a growth from the same root, we need not wonder at the zeal and earnestness with which it hath very lately been treated by a learned and able prelate of this Church, *whose words are the words of wisdom, and his example worthy of imitation.*" (*Charge*, 1792, p. 19.) The generality of the evil thus stands recorded on this high authority, confirmed also by that of Archbishop Secker, already given in the following words :—" THE TRUTH, I fear, is, that *many*, if NOT MOST OF US, have dwelt too little on these doctrines in our sermons," . . . and " *the effect has been lamentable.*" *Most lamentable indeed!* " Our people have grown less and less mindful, FIRST, of the *distinguishing* articles of their creed, THEN, *as will always be the case*, of that one which they hold, *in common with the heathens.*"

This, then, being the *heathenish*, or worse than heathenish state, from which, according to the authority of Archbishop Secker, Bishop Horsley, and Bishop Horne, we have been rescued, it becomes us to ponder well by what instrumentality chiefly, under God, the mighty change has been effected. And few will have the hardihood to deny THE FACT, that it has been accomplished chiefly by the foolishness of preaching: by the simple preaching of the cross of Christ by men of the stamp of Romaine, Hervey, Milner, Venn, Berridge, Robinson, Newton, Serle, Scott, Cecil, Simeon—men who ever repudiated the High Church dogmas which we have been considering; who preached " Christ crucified," not " the Sacraments," for salvation ; who, instead of directing their hearers to be "*as sure*" of the Bishops being Christ's representatives as if they saw them exercising miraculous gifts, and describing those preachers of the Gospel who followed not them, as treading in the footsteps and partaking of the judgment of Korah and his company, embraced with brotherly affection, after the example of our venerable reformers and martyrs, all other Churches who held the Head, and united cordially with Bishop Hall in denominating them "the dear spouse of Christ."

It was such men as we have named, and who were far from being in the high places of the Church, or remarkably distinguished, generally speaking, for this world's qualifications, whom it pleased God, who doeth all things according to the counsel of His will, to employ, as his instruments, for the awakening of the slumbering Church. They were the seed of the Church. And what a harvest has the seed of that generation produced! Ye see, brethren, how many thousands of the clergy, instead of losing sight of "their proper office," or being merely "the apes of Epictetus," preach with all boldness the peculiar doctrines of the Gospel to the salvation of myriads; while even those who revolt at and nauseate this statement, who see no beauty nor glory in this mighty change, who think the Church was incomparably better as she was before, previous to the appearance of "those troublers of Israel," have been forced by a power they could not withstand, and an example they have been constrained to follow, to raise and Christianize the tone and matter of their preaching. Far indeed, is it from being what it ought to be, but *the reflection* of the light of the pure Gospel shining around them, is now to be discerned in every parish of the land.

Such worthies as we have named and their successors have delivered over to the men of this generation a sacred deposit to keep—a deposit of incomparable value, and on the preservation of which in its entireness and purity is hung suspended the destiny of millions yet unborn. This inestimable treasure is the pure, unsophisticated Gospel of the kingdom, which they themselves preached with the astonishing results which we this day see. They preached it amidst reproach, contumely, and scorn, but they preached on. The names which the Rev. Dr. Crofts applied to them, are nothing more nor less than the appellations with which they were generally honoured, and these were such as the following:—"Fanatical Divines," "Clerical Enthusiasts," "Pretended favourites of Heaven." They have served their generation and fallen asleep. Now is our day—now are we called to like faithfulness under circumstances in many respects dissimilar, but not less trying *to our integrity*.

Such attacks on the preachers of Evangelical truth as have recently appeared in the *British Critic*, are not now-a-days common, nor are they favoured by the higher and more respectable classes in the Church. Not a few men of sound spiritual religion are now being advanced to the higher places of the Church, and their state is gradually changing from the wholesome one of persecution, to the far more dangerous condition of prosperity. The temptation now presented to many, is to moderate and smooth the tone of their preaching, so that they may not be (in so far as their principles will possibly admit) *marked men*, and so be prevented from rising to places of higher elevation and, of course, as they are very forward to admit, of greater usefulness; and again, there are those principles of High Churchmanship which we have been considering, presented to them with the high inducement we have just named, and earnestly recommended by men of great talents and learning, of high character and station—principles, which, of all others, are captivating to the natural heart of man, and to which the present aspect of the times and of the Church give a peculiar point and effect.

In such circumstances we are called upon to "hold fast our integrity." To swerve not to the right hand or to the left. Not to be "ignorant of Satan's devices." To remember the fair garbs which he assumes for the accomplishment of his purposes, even "transforming himself into an angel of light." To remember that "the offence of the cross" has not ceased: that if we are the true and genuine and *open* servants of our Lord, we must be content to be, like Him, despised and rejected: that if we have become thoroughly respected by the world, we have much cause to doubt our principles, or our fidelity. We are called upon to bear in mind the vanity and evanescent character of all earthly things, of all human favour, and all earthly glory: how vain is the honour that cometh from man; how rich and everlasting that which cometh from God only. To think of the dishonour and turpitude of defeat, the glories and rewards of victory. To listen to the words of our Lord, " *Hold that fast which thou hast, that no man take thy crown.*"

We know full well that such statements expose those who make them to the anger and hostility of such as consider themselves aggrieved by them. But truth is truth. The rule is, that it should be known —the exception, that it should be concealed; and in the present case, we are persuaded, there is no sufficient ground for concealment; on the contrary, strong reasons that it should be declared. Hannah Moore says, in her *Strictures on Education*, " so to expose the weakness of the land, as to suggest the necessity of internal improvement, and to point out the means of effectual defence, is not *treachery*, but *patriotism.*" And if the truth of such a statement be admitted, as applied to worldly things, how much more when it refers to things spiritual and eternal. Inconvenience may attend the exposure, but if it is conducive to the preservation and establishment of the truth, it may be well endured.

THE END.

Macintosh, Printer, 20, Great New Street, London.